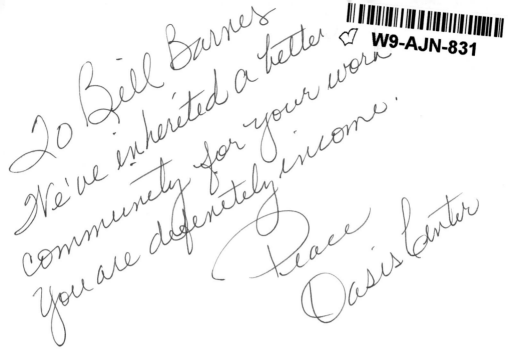

To Bill Barnes
We've inherited a better
community for your work.
You are defenetely income.
Peace
Oasis Center

Person-Centered
LEADERSHIP for NONPROFIT ORGANIZATIONS

Person-Centered

LEADERSHIP for NONPROFIT ORGANIZATIONS

Management That Works in High Pressure Systems

Jeanne M. Plas
Susan E. Lewis

Sage Publications
International Educational and Professional Publisher
Thousand Oaks ■ London ■ New Delhi

For information:

Sage Publications, Inc.
2455 Teller Road
Thousand Oaks, California 91320
E-mail: order@sagepub.com

Sage Publications Ltd.
6 Bonhill Street
London EC2A 4PU
United Kingdom

Sage Publications India Pvt. Ltd.
M-32 Market
Greater Kailash I
New Delhi 110 048 India

Printed in the United States of America

Library of Congress Cataloging-in-Publication Data

Plas, Jeanne M.

Person-centered leadership for nonprofit organizations: Management that works in
   high pressure systems / by Jeanne M. Plas and Susan E. Lewis.
      p. cm.
   Includes bibliographical references and index.
   ISBN 0-7619-0624-X (cloth: acid-free paper)
      1. Nonprofit organizations—United States—Management.
2. Leadership. 3. Management—Employee participation.
I. Lewis, Susan E. II. Title.
   HD62.6 .P63 2000
   658.3'152—dc21   00-011705

01   02   03   04   05   06   10   9   8   7   6   5   4   3   2   1

Acquiring Editor:	Jim Brace-Thompson
Editorial Assistant:	Anna Howland
Production Editor:	Nevair Kabakian
Editorial Assistant:	Candice Crosetti
Typesetter/Designer:	D&G Limited
Indexer:	D&G Limited
Cover Designer:	Michelle Lee

Contents

Preface   vii

Part I   Participatory Management and the Challenges of   1
         Nonprofit Organizations: The Past, the Future,
         and Person-Centered Possibilities

         Introduction   3

         1. Survival Within Today's Nonprofit Organizations: 5
            Pressures and Burnout

         2. Possibilities in Participatory Management   19

         3. Person-Centered Leadership   35

Part II A Person-Centered, Nonprofit Example of Excellence   47

         Introduction   49

         4. Oasis Center: An Overview   51

         5. The Oasis Person-Centered Model   63

         6. Strengths and Weaknesses: Growing Pains and   95
            Growing Satisfactions

         7. The Board of Directors: The Creation of a New   123
            Participatory Model

         8. The Shelter: Against All Odds   133

         9. A Vital and Vibrant Infrastructure: Teamwork   147
            That Works

        10. The Future of Nonprofit Participatory Management   159

         Appendix: Methods   167

         Index   169

         About the Authors   175

Dedication

This work is dedicated to all the
Oasis Center personnel we have known.
These individuals trust the future.
They are helping to create it.
We are deeply grateful for all the hopeful lessons learned.

Preface

Years before corporate organizations discovered the strength of participatory-management models, parts of many nonprofit organizations as diverse in scope as the San Diego Zoo and the American Red Cross were successfully using some of these management strategies (c.f., Hamilton & Tragert, 1998). Yet, despite the early history of some nonprofit organizations, it has been the for-profit sector that has embraced these models in the most fundamental and sweeping ways. Finding a corporation of any size today that has not implemented at least portions of a participatory-management model is difficult. Indeed, most start-up companies, especially in the technology arena, are heavy users of participatory rather than top-down management. Where this sort of lateral management has been successful, companies have reported increased quality, production, and revenue while identifying significant reductions in benchmarks such as turnover rates (Plas, 1996; Segil, 1999; & Tichy, 1997). For nonprofit personnel, the most provocative aspect of all of this participatory-management modeling might well be the growing number of intriguing stories of increased employee morale and reduction of organizational stress.

Nonprofit organizations are well-known pressure cookers. With difficult goals, needy clientele, and under-resourced budgets and buildings, nonprofit professionals have been particularly vulnerable to issues of burnout (Maslach, 1997). Participatory-management strategies might hold the key to stress reduction among staff professionals in nonprofit organizations. This book presents evidence of that through the discussion of a five-year study of a participatory nonprofit organization—a social-service agency that began les ago as an oasis for troubled youth. Now, the organization has mission, can describe impressive credentials and results, and is relatively free of the outcomes that are usually associated with staff burnout. Everyone involved credits the participatory leadership and management strategy that has been solidly in place there for about 15 years.

We describe the leadership and management strategies used by this award-winning social-service agency in Part Two of this book. Within that narrative, we introduce the organization, focus on its structure, and carefully describe the particular strategies that have been used successfully there since the mid 1980s.

In Part One, prior to introducing the case study, we engage the issues surrounding participatory management and identify its potential for nonprofit organizations that are caught in crisis as a result of decreased staff size, overwhelming caseload demands, inadequate funding, and sometimes poor communication within the community and within the organization. Among the important issues that we talk about in Part One are the differences between leadership and management as well as the success and failure scenarios that many organizations, predominately for-profit entities, have experienced with participatory leadership and management.

PERSON-CENTERED LEADERSHIP

The central focus of this book is a certain kind of participatory management called *person-centered leadership*. In this form of participatory management, regard for the employee is as deep as the regard for the client, service, and product. Person-centered leadership requires a great deal of attention to be given to individual employees, be they professionals, support staff, or board members. This participatory approach seems to show especially good promise for successful use in today's nonprofit organizations. The agency that you will read about in Part Two relies exclusively on a person-centered approach to leadership, management, and strategic planning.

INTENDED AUDIENCE AND FORMAT

Person-Centered Leadership for Nonprofit Organizations was written with the professional practitioner in mind. Our primary audience is composed of those many thousands of people who are committed to nonprofit organizations and the work that goes on at those agencies. Under this umbrella, we include caseworkers, administrators, office and budgetary personnel, board members, fundraisers, funding organizations, and liaison personnel of all sorts. A secondary audience of special importance is the university-based student of nonprofit leadership and practice. The book was designed for both audiences.

The format we use grew from a common understanding that these two audiences have somewhat different reading agendas. The field practitioner of today typically wants a clear and somewhat enthusiastic description of solid and new approaches to the job at hand. Commonly, practitioners are juggling heavy workloads with built-in stressors at the same time that they are balancing home, family, and personal community commitments. So, for many field-based personnel, a useful book of the sort presented here has to contain clear descriptions, but it also has to connect directly to the issues that the reader is likely to encounter each day. Easily accessed lists of strategies and next steps also are often appreciated by those in our primary audience. In contrast, while student groups tend to be equally interested in ideas and implementations, they are not as likely to want information in any sort of urgent way. Typically, readers within this audience are not in a position to need help with an on-the-job problem. Rather, a student reader more often needs to know how the material connects to other sorts of information and perspectives that they have been learning. Thus, while references to a variety of other writings might slow down the field-practitioner reader, such references are typically important for the student.

Despite a somewhat different emphasis on literature citations, both audiences tend to respond well to a careful case-study approach. A case study helps the seasoned practitioner relate daily stresses, successes, and failures to those that are experienced by others who work within similar organizations. Almost intuitively, practitioners evaluate the worth of an idea or strategy based on personal experience in the field. In counterpoint, one of the university professor's greatest challenges is how to effectively teach material to students who might not have the sort of personal experience that can be so useful in evaluating content. A case-study approach can often provide exactly the sort of step-by-step information that bridges this gap for the student.

The format that we use here is designed to respond to the needs of both audiences. While Part Two highlights the case study rather than the literature, we provide basic references to other research and thinking throughout Part One. Thus, the discussions in Part One provide literature-based development of important topics for those readers who want to linger with a theme, connecting the ideas to issues and examples raised by other writers and researchers. Those readers who want to more quickly press on to the case study description might choose to read through some of the earlier discussions with less attention to detail and to the citations.

The Book

The book is divided into two major sections. Chapters 1, 2, and 3 in Part One discuss nonprofit organizational realities, participatory management, person-centered leadership, and the potential of this model for nonprofit goals. While some references to the case-study organization can be found in these chapters, they are primarily intended to provide an overview of the general possibilities that this sort of leadership and management can maximize within today's nonprofit organizations. Those who are already familiar with participatory and person-centered leadership might want to move directly to Part Two, where we describe the agency story. Part One, the intellectual core of the book, provides the context within which to consider the case study organization's project in participatory management.

Part Two constitutes the heart of the book. Here, within Chapters 4 through 9, we introduce this exemplary social-service organization, The Oasis Center. We illustrate its unique person-centered leadership structure and style and provide examples that illustrate the way things work at Oasis. Having described the Oasis person-centered model in Chapters 4 and 5, we describe the organization's resulting weaknesses and strengths in Chapter 6, and we discuss the board's functioning in Chapter 7. We illustrate how this participatory-management system translates into action in Chapters 8 and 9, which cover a specific program, the shelter, and a part of the infrastructure, teams, and team-building. Bridges to Practice are scattered throughout these chapters. A concluding chapter outlines important lessons that we have learned throughout our study of the issues and the case-study organization.

ABOUT OUR RESEARCH, COLLABORATION, AND APPROACH TO THIS BOOK

This book was written in a style that is compatible with a person-centered approach. We often focus on individuals as we report results and offer interpretations. We tend to write in the first person when that makes sense. We try to stay constantly mindful of you, the reader. At times, this approach has been a bit awkward to deliver. For example, when one of us is relating a conversation and it seems that greater narrative validity can be achieved if we write in the first person, we are cognizant that you are unaware of which of us is speaking at that time. After discussing and discarding various ways of approaching this problem, we finally decided simply to assume that the issue of which one is speaking is actually irrelevant to the message and that readers would not be unduly distracted by the absence of that information. If our method of handling this issue creates problems, we apologize and beg your indulgence.

The Collaboration

As an introduction to our collaboration, we offer a brief introduction of ourselves as individuals at this point. Jeanne Plas, the senior author, has studied person-centered corporate organizations throughout the 1990s. As an author of two books that discuss participatory-management strategies and report results of her studies of person-centered organizations (Arnold & Plas, 1993; & Plas, 1996), she has been called on to consult with corporate organizations in the United States, Europe, and Canada. Plas has been a teacher and researcher at Vanderbilt University for the past 25 years, where she has primarily been affiliated with the community-clinical doctoral training program. During the past dozen years, she has restricted her scholarly interests to leadership research and related issues, such as the phenomenon of sense of community.

Having left nonprofit management work to return to school, the second author, Susan Lewis, has recently finished her dissertation within the Community Psychology program at Vanderbilt University. Her research and writing efforts have been directed toward nonprofit management as well as issues related to sense of community. As a result of Lewis's former experience as an executive director of an international nonprofit organization, throughout the 1990s she has been an organizational consultant to nonprofit boards and professional associations.

During the mid and late '90s, as corporate organizations were giving enormous amounts of attention to participatory-management strategies, it often struck each of us as odd that nonprofit literature and practice seemed relatively bereft of discussions of landmark quality-improvement and participatory-management issues. During a year when Lewis was doing a community psychology internship at The Oasis Center and Plas was contributing to a small consultation project there, we put our heads together, wondering aloud about this lack of literature attention. One of us brought to the project expertise in participatory-management research and consultation—especially person-centered approaches—while the other brought to the table expertise in general nonprofit management and consultation. Thus, the dual foci of the longitudinal study reported here were represented within our interests at the outset of the project.

The Research Project

A commitment to a person-centered leadership philosophy has been more than obvious at Oasis, the case-study organization. Its reputation in the community and nationally has been impeccable for quite some time. Therefore, we approached this organization about the possibility of studying it in order to learn several things. Among them, we hoped to find answers to the questions, "Is this a thoroughly participatory organization, or is the philosophy more surface than core?" "Is person-centered leadership, rather than merely management, in place?" "What leadership and management strategies have produced the best outcomes?"

Because Oasis is a reflective organization, the group became intrigued with the possibility that our investigation might unearth weaknesses and/or faults that would be useful for them to know. Being a participatory organization, however, meant that people throughout Oasis needed to have a chance to endorse the project prior to the project becoming full scale and receiving final approval. Thus began a five-year longitudinal study. After a hiatus of about 18 months subsequent to the study's primary year-long data-collection phase, we collected follow-up data across a three-month period. A year after that, we again went to the agency for follow-up. A fourth stage of data collection occurred a year beyond the third.

Methods

The methodological approach used in this study was largely qualitative. Inspired by the methodological work of Lincoln and Guba (1985) and others (Argyris, 1990; Jick, 1979; & Kirk & Miller, 1986), the project depended on a triangulation strategy that used three distinct stages. Question construction/sampling was followed by inductive analysis and theory development, which resulted in a reconstructed methodological plan. The research process continually cycled through these stages. That is, tentative hypotheses led us logically to certain samples, where data were gathered and then analyzed. New theoretical interpretations resulted and new samples and data were gathered, and so on through the cycle again. Additional instructions to this technique will be found in Part Two and in the Appendix.

WHAT IS A NONPROFIT ORGANIZATION?

We recognize the conventional definition of a nonprofit organization to refer to groups that do not generate revenue in excess of expenses as profit (the so-called non-distributive constraint). There are many types of nonprofit organizations; among them are social-service agencies, trade or professional organizations, and religious groups. Throughout this book, we often include government agencies in our thinking, because while not typically categorized as nonprofit organizations, people who work within local, state, and federal units often share some of the same concerns with those who work within mainstream nonprofit organizations.

Social-service agencies are mission-oriented organizations that are board or community mandated to respond to a particular community or national need that is most often related to a human-development issue or crisis of some sort. Most often, sources of funding for this sort of agency include dues, grants, fees, and donations from businesses, individuals, and philanthropic foundations. Government agencies, on the other hand, are charged with administering the laws, rules, and regulations established by local, state, and federal bodies. The source of funding is tax based. A third category of nonprofit organization, the trade or professional organization, is growing in importance and in number these days. A professional nonprofit group is most often concerned with enhancing the profession's identity, refining its mission, and providing internal quality control of its members. These groups also tend to engage in legislative lobbying efforts to effect laws regarding the industry or profession. This type of nonprofit organization is commonly funded by dues paid by its membership.

The common denominator for all types of nonprofit organizations is that funding in excess of expenses (i.e., profit) is not expected to be distributed. The differences among these types of nonprofit organizations can be large. In this book, the focus is primarily on social-service organizations, although the lessons learned can be applicable to a variety of professional organizations, as well. While government organizations are not the sort of nonprofit organizations that we primarily target, it is also clear that some government organizations have attempted to maximize their potential by using participatory-management methods (for example, the United States Postal Service).

The reader should be aware that we use the terms *nonprofit organization* and *social-service agency* interchangeably throughout the book, because our case study is a social-service agency. Nonetheless, the principles articulated here and the strategies that are discussed can be conceivably of interest also to those who work within professional organizations, government offices, and agencies.

ENTHUSIASM AND OBJECTIVITY

As researchers, we are constantly aware of our obligation, desire, and commitment to approach data with caution and with a certain amount of reasoned objectivity. Typically, the methodology that a researcher uses is expected to provide this sort of objectivity at the same time that it structures things so that solid data can be collected in response to research questions and issues. In fact, a researcher's personal, detached objectivity is often as valuable as the methodology that is employed. Such was the case with our research project at Oasis, the agency we write about in the second portion of this book. At the outset, we adopted a dispassionate orientation to the organization and developed a methodology that was capable of revealing the realities within it. We must advise the reader, however, that at the close of the multi-year project described in the case study, our objectivity was compromised for an important reason: We had come to learn just how stellar this organization is. Our initial scientific lack of passion for this organization turned to obvious enthusiasm.

In the following pages, while attempting to convey the quality of this organization, we at times share with you the excitement that we developed about it and the possibilities that it represents for nonprofit leadership in the 21st century. To pretend at this point to own the objectivity we initially experienced throughout the first years of the Oasis project would be to mislead the reader. We believe that the integrity of the research project is best protected by admitting at this point that we are impressed with this organization in fundamental ways.

We studied this organization carefully for several years, stepping away from it for 10 to 12 months at a time, then returning with fresh perspective and objectivity. Each time, we came away impressed. The reader will note our high regard for this organization throughout the description of the case study. We hope that this description honestly adds to, rather than detracts from, the reader's understanding.

REFERENCES

Argyris, C. (1990). *Overcoming organizational defenses.* Boston: Allyn & Bacon.

Arnold, W. W. and Plas, J. M. (1993). *The human touch: Today's most unusual program for productivity and profit.* New York: John Wiley & Sons, Inc.

Hamilton, L. and Tragert, R. (1998). *100 best nonprofits to work for: Find your dream job and launch a rewarding career doing good!* New York: Beach Brook Productions.

Jick, T. D. (1979). Mixing qualitative and quantitative methods: Triangulation in action. *Administrative Science Quarterly*, Volume 24, pp. 602–611.

Kirk, J. and Miller, M. L. (1986). *Reliability and validity in qualitative research.* Beverly Hills, CA: Sage Publications, Inc.

Lincoln, Y. S. and Guba, E. (1985). *Naturalistic inquiry.* Beverly Hills, CA: Sage Publications, Inc.

Maslach, C. and Leiter, M. P. (1997). *The truth about burnout: How organizations cause personal stress and what to do about it.* San Francisco: Jossey-Bass.

Plas, J. M. (1996). *Person-centered leadership: An American approach to participatory management.* Thousand Oaks, CA: Sage Publications, Inc.

Segil, L. (1999). Great leadership. *Executive Excellence*, Volume 16(9), pp. 54–61.

Tichy, N. M. (1997). *The leadership engine: How winning companies build leaders at every level.* New York: Harper Business.

PART I

Participatory Management and the Challenges of Nonprofit Organizations

The Past, the Future, and Person-Centered Possibilities

INTRODUCTION

A revolution is underway in organizational management. In growing numbers, organizations—especially corporate entities—have turned toward participatory management systems that emphasize quality improvement, employee empowerment, and executives who serve (Greenleaf, 1998; Hesselbein, Goldsmith, & Berkhard, 1996; & Yukl, 1998). Corporate America is learning how to create better quality and greater profit by increasing regard for the individual front-line worker—the person who has the real expertise and who is, ultimately, the major factor in completing any quality job. These newer participatory management approaches have improved productivity and profit while increasing worker satisfaction and well-being. As we demonstrate throughout this book, in recent years these approaches have proven to be clearly more than just passing fads.

Yet, relatively few social-service organizations have used these management models to a great extent. (For good examples of typical, traditional management models that nonprofit organizations currently use, refer to Herman & Heimovics, 1991; & Letts, Ryan, & Grossman, 1999. For a comprehensive look at past and present leadership theories, refer to Clegg, Hardy, & Nord, eds., 1996.) Despite the intriguing possibility that success stories could be even greater for service organizations than they have been for corporate entities, a surprisingly small number of nonprofit organizations have adopted so-called participatory management and leadership strategies. Person-centered leadership, an approach to participatory management that has been shown to be impressively effective in United States and other western organizational cultures (Arnold & Plas, 1993; & Plas, 1996) seems uniquely suited for use in a variety of nonprofit settings. A few social-service organizations have begun to implement structural and management models that have obvious person-centered components.

Later in this book, we report a full-scale person-centered implementation story that emerged from an extensive qualitative research project. This success story is of impressive proportions. Before we turn our attention toward this story, however, we need to provide the context into which it fits.

Understanding the possibilities of nonprofit leadership and management that are inherent in person-centered leadership requires us to first consider two basic issues: the current climate within which nonprofit organizations attempt to survive and advance, and the history and current uses of those strategies that are now called participatory management. In Chapter 1, we discuss the pressures and goals of today's social-service organizations. Here, we give special attention to the issue of burnout, a phenomenon that has plagued a large number of nonprofit organizations and that we will later show is likely to be impacted when certain types of participatory management are in place. In Chapter 2, we provide an overview of participatory management models and talk about issues such as the differences between leadership and management. Chapter 3 discusses person-centered leadership, its unique and contrasting characteristics, and its potential for success within nonprofit organizations.

REFERENCES

Arnold, W. W. and Plas, J. M. (1993). *The human touch: Today's most unusual program for productivity and profit.* New York: John Wiley & Sons, Inc.

Greenleaf, R. K. (1998). *The power of servant leadership.* San Francisco: Barrett-Koehler.

Herman, R. D. and Heimovics, R. D. (1991). *Executive leadership in nonprofit organizations.* San Francisco: Jossey-Bass.

Hesselbein, F.; Goldsmith, M., and Beckhard, R. (1996). *The leader of the future.* San Francisco: Jossey-Bass.

Letts, C. W., Ryan, W. P., and Grossman, A. (1999). *High performance nonprofit organizations.* New York: John Wiley & Sons, Inc.

Mason, D. (1996). *Leading and managing the expressive dimension.* San Francisco: Jossey-Bass.

Plas, J. M. (1996). *Person-centered leadership: An American approach to participatory management.* Thousand Oaks, CA: Sage Publications, Inc.

Steckel, R. and Lehman, J. (1997). *In search of America's best nonprofits.* San Francisco: Jossey-Bass.

Yukl, G. (1998). *Leadership in organizations* (4th ed.). Upper Saddle River, NJ: Prentice Hall.

1

Survival Within Today's Nonprofit Organizations

Pressures and Burnout

SERVICE PROVIDERS: THE PRESSURES AND COSTS

He knew from friends at school what the bright yellow Safe Place signs meant. He had seen them all over town—at McDonald's, the grocery store, Blockbuster, and even on MTA buses. "If you're in trouble, we can help," Daryl recalled. He knew he was in trouble, and he decided to see if it would work.

Daryl entered a store sporting the Safe Place logo and asked for help. Without a question, a quick call to Oasis Center provided Daryl a ride to their youth shelter. He arrived with the clothes on his back—torn jeans that sagged on his youthful frame; an *N Sync tee shirt dirtied from three days of constant wear; and a worn military-style jacket.

Oasis policy required a call to Daryl's mother, whom he considered the root of the problem. He was tired of her beatings. She would hit him with a belt, take a smoke break, and start in again. He was angry, and acted out in wild and unacceptable ways—some of them personally harmful (drugs) and some illegal (theft and vandalism). Daryl wasn't just in trouble. In his own words, he was in "deep trouble."

Daryl's mother was glad he was in the shelter, and quickly gave her permission for him to stay. One of the few things Daryl and his mother had ever agreed upon was that he was now an Oasis problem.

It may be that only people who have worked for or with nonprofit organizations—youth shelters, counseling centers, departments of human services, legal aid, rescue missions, and so forth—can truly understand the nature of the unique pressures associated with simply getting up to go to work somewhere within America's vast labyrinth of agencies. Daryl is the kind of person who is the target of all the efforts. As a symbol of the poor, the disabled, the raped, and the wronged, he's the point of it all.

Daryl's problems are complex. They are severe. They are historically entrenched within his family system and the community systems in which he participates. People who go to work each day in the social service sector are paid—quite simply—to make a difference in all of this chaos. Society expects them to change things; if not, to quietly manage them; or, in the absence of either, to at least get the problems off the streets. Failing all of the above, we're usually willing to at least settle for a little hope. We want these workers, these mere human beings, to create hope—for all the victims and for those of us who observe victims' pain and want a cessation of the agonies.

Typical social service workers deal with huge sets of expectations—their society's, their clients', their employer's, and their own. These expectation burdens typically rival or exceed those of the most beleaguered middle managers and senior executives charged with creating product, market share, and revenue in today's internationally competitive corporate world.

We want Daryl's social worker, or his counselor, or his juvenile justice probation officer to change his world. If they can't do that, we want somebody to get Daryl a good family therapist, or a great emergency shelter—or, maybe we'd be relieved if somebody would just get him a decent part-time job. Depending on who's doing the asking, there will be requests that Daryl's mother get counseling, or get jailed, or get just plain "fixed," somehow. Yet, when we push ourselves to consider Daryl's problems at their most basic level, we realize that what we really want is for both Daryl and his mother to feel safe, to respect themselves, to love one another, to work, laugh, share and be happy. Whatever the symptoms are, most of the time it boils down to just that. Ultimately, we want our social service personnel to work the miracle of getting Daryl and his mother (and whomever else is part of the family system) to genuinely like and respect themselves, because that sort of healthy sense of self is the stuff of which good families and jobs and communities are made.

So, make no mistake about it. We want miracles. A standard dictionary defines a miracle as "an accomplishment or occurrence so outstanding or unusual as to seem beyond human capability or endeavor." By this definition, if any social service agency were to actually help Daryl and his mother solve their complex and painful problems, we would grant them the status of miracle worker. All the situations to which we allude here—the battering, malnutrition, disability, and hate—are so complex and so difficult that we lose heart and lose hope. Society is overwhelmed by its social burdens and we are left to pray on the one hand, and to expect on the other, that the social service workers we hire to solve these problems will routinely create the miracles that we know we so desperately need.

But, what is the effect of these societal expectations on an individual nonprofit employee? We are coming to learn that the effects are tremendous. Uncomfortable issues associated with burnout, low status, and poor compensation packages are ubiquitous within our nonprofit sectors. Social service workers often report high stress levels, feelings of inadequacy, and little job satisfaction. In many cases, people leave nonprofit careers and jobs at a higher rate than in other fields.

BURNOUT

History and Definition

The study of burnout began in the early 1970s with the observations of a clinical psychologist working at a drop-in center for drug addicts in New York City. Herbert Freudenberger (1974, 1975) noted that a great proportion of the young and idealistic counselors working at the center soon appeared as if they themselves were in great distress. Feeling challenged by the enormity of the task and the seemingly insatiable neediness of their clients, these counselors would work harder and harder to succeed, stopping only at the point of near-total exhaustion. Freudenberger borrowed the term burnout, which was used to describe the effects of chronic drug use, and applied this term to the service providers (Maslach & Schaufeli, 1993).

At about the same time, Christina Maslach (1976), a social-psychology researcher, was studying ways in which people cope with emotional arousal on the job, such as detached concern and dehumanization in self-defense. When she described her findings to an attorney, she was told that poverty lawyers call this phenomenon burnout.

Burnout thus began more as commentary on a social phenomenon rather than as an empirically derived academic concept. In fact, in those early years, the concept was not openly discussed because it seemed tantamount to admitting that professionals can act unprofessional. Many chose to believe that such a phenomenon was surely limited to a small minority

(Maslach, 1993). During the 1980s, the work on burnout entered a more focused, constructive, and empirical period, and a widely-used operational definition now exists that includes three components: 1) depersonalization, 2) reduced personal accomplishment, and 3) emotional exhaustion. Depersonalization refers to a negative, callous, or excessively detached response to other people, particularly recipients of the provider's service or care. Reduced personal accomplishment refers to a decline in one's feelings of competence and successful achievement in one's work. Emotional exhaustion refers to feelings of being emotionally overextended and depleted of one's emotional resources (Maslach).

Golembiewshi, Munzenrider, and Carter (1983) suggest that the components of burnout develop in a linear and progressive manner (refer to Figure 1.1). Depersonalization is considered the initial burnout phase. Treating people as objects can lead to a diminished sense of personal accomplishment (and thus, diminished personal involvement). When depersonalization and diminished personal accomplishment take hold, the stage becomes set for some tragic cycling that can escalate to severe emotional exhaustion. Freudenberger (1974, pp. 160–162) describes the following symptoms that provide a graphic sense of this self-reinforcing cycle:

"... quickness to anger and ... instantaneous irritation and frustration ... "
; ... the person becomes the 'house cynic' ... [and] blocks progress and constructive change ... because change means another adaptation [for which] he is just too tired ... ; " the person spends "a greater and greater number of physical hours [at work], but less and less is being accomplished"; and the person desperately needs support and caring but, often because of an intensified preoccupation with work and lengthening hours, the individual "has just about lost most of his friends."

	Diminished	Diminished	
Depersonalized →	Personal →	Personal →	Emotional
	Accomplishment	Involvement	Exhaustion

Figure 1.1.   Progression of the Burnout Cycle

NOTE: From *Phases of progressive burnout and their work site covariants: Critical issues in OD research and praxis*, by R. T. Golembiewshi, R. Munzenrider, and D. Carter, 1983, *The Journal of Applied Behavioral Science*, Volume 19, p. 480. Copyright 1983 by Sage Publications, Inc.

Research Findings

Several early longitudinal studies of burnout (Dignam & West, 1988; Firth & Britton, 1989; Jackson, Schwab, & Schuler, 1986; & Wade, Cooley, & Savicki, 1986) established three major conclusions. First, burnout levels within organizations tend to be fairly stable over time, reflecting a more chronic than acute phenomenon. Second, role conflict and lack of social support from colleagues and supervisors are antecedents of burnout. Third, burnout leads to physical symptoms, absenteeism, and job turnover.

A more recent longitudinal study (Mirvis, Graney, & Osborne-Kilpatrick, 1999) is comparable to the earlier studies in that it uses the same Maslach model and measures of burnout. Findings support the latter two assertions regarding antecedents and the resulting behaviors of burnout. The Mirvis study, however, reflected a dramatic 78 percent increase in moderate or high levels of burnout over an eight-year study period of leaders of the *Department of Veterans Affairs* (VA). This finding is consistent with the idea that burnout is chronic, rather than acute; however, it also suggests (at least, in this sample) that burnout is becoming worse over time.

Maslach, who helped coin the term burnout in the 1970s, concurs from a broader perspective (Maslach & Leiter, 1997), having devoted a 20-year career to the subject. She and her co-author suggest six reasons for increased burnout:

- Work overload—Having too much to do in too little time takes form in both current jobs that have increased demands and in those employees who take on second jobs, as well.

  - Lack of control—People want enough autonomy to make their own decisions and solve problems. Policies that restrict individual creativity diminish this capacity and foster burnout.

  - Lack of reward—Verbal and emotional recognition is more important than monetary rewards. The loss of internal rewards when a job is well done and is not recognized is most devastating.

- Lack of community—People need a positive connection with others in the workplace. Sometimes technology makes social contact impersonal, but what is most destructive to a sense of community is unresolved conflict. According to Maslach, conflict tears apart the fabric of social support, making support in difficult times less likely.

Taking a social-psychological perspective, Geurts, Schaufeli, and DeJonge (1998) emphasize that burnout can take either a behavioral withdrawal (an intention to leave, for example) or a psychological withdrawal (feelings of depersonalization, for example). Germane to the current work, this study was conducted among mental health-care professionals with a subsample from a residential facility. Results found that thoughts about leaving the organization were often triggered by negative communication with colleagues about management.

Indeed, in some health fields, turnover rates are alarming. Barrett, Riggar, Flowers, Crimando, and Bailey (1997) cite average turnover rates in community rehabilitation centers as 18.3 percent for supervisory management and 28.6 percent for direct service staff. The authors translate these data into estimates of actual financial costs ranging from $128,217 to $201,600 annually. This expense conservatively accounts for financial losses due to mistakes and confusion, systems disarray, disruptions in client programming, and decreased staff morale, resulting in lost productivity and new staffing costs. The Barrett study suggests two factors relating directly to rehabilitation leadership: management and supervision (which might account for the continuing high levels of rehabilitation-personnel turnover).

First, the researchers note that approximately 75 percent of rehabilitation administrators have had little or no education or training concerning management and administration. Masters-level counselors are promoted to supervisory positions on the average within 14.25 months following graduation. Not only do these supervisors have no management training, but they have had only brief exposure to institutional protocol even as counselors.

Second, interview data demonstrate that management groups view the "why" personnel leave considerably differently than do those who actually leave. Managers and supervisors do not feel burnout at the same intense rates as direct service providers and find morale an intangible concept that is difficult to quantify. Those who left, however, were clear about their reasons for doing so: little advancement potential (achievement and recognition), little job satisfaction (dissatisfaction, self-esteem, distress, policy, and administration), stress burnout (lack of personal accomplishment, depersonalization, and emotional exhaustion), and personality differences with management/supervision (lack of direction, support, consideration, and attitudes).

In a survey of 254 nursing homes, Banaszak-Holl and Hines (1996) found turnover rates among nursing aides averaging 32 percent in a six-month period, although they cite previous studies finding the average turnover rate as high as 75 percent. Similar to the rehabilitation workers, nursing aides reported the highest levels of dissatisfaction with communication and structure of work. Job design factors, such as flexibility, involvement with decision making, and employee training were cited as most important for work satisfaction.

Strategies for Prevention

The studies suggest that preventive or corrective measures for burnout might be approached from two perspectives: personal and organizational. We believe that these approaches are not mutually exclusive. Some authors (Jevne & Williams, 1998; & Stevens, 1995) suggest that when an individual feels symptoms of burnout, he or she should appropriately take corrective individual measures. Maslach and Leiter (1997) argue, however, that burnout is not ultimately a problem of the individual worker; rather, they argue that the problem is related to the social environment in which people work. The focus of this book highlights the organizational changes that can assist in that endeavor.

Numerous researchers have found support for a variety of strategies to prevent or at least diminish burnout. Barrett, Crimando, and Riggar (1993) detail the process of becoming an empowering organization through trust, open communication, beliefs and expectations, and organizational structure and physical arrangements. In another study, these same authors (1995) emphasize continuous performance appraisal in non-adversarial and empowering relationships. Krakinowski (1992) highlights the need to address staff caseloads, offer support, say thank you, and provide employee-assistance programs.

In reviewing her 15-year program of research on burnout, Cary Cherniss (1993) uses Bandura's (1977, 1982) work on self-efficacy to understand effective buffers against professional burnout. Cherniss notes that self-efficacy is not a global concept and that a person can feel efficacious in one kind of role or setting but not in another. She identifies three domains in which self-efficacy is important: 1) the task domain, 2) the interpersonal domain, and 3) the organizational domain. The task domain focuses on the professional skills and competencies that an individual brings to the job. The second domain relates to a person's ability to work harmoniously with others, including clients, co-workers, and supervisors. The third domain, which Cherniss claims is the most critical, refers to beliefs about one's ability to influence social and political forces within the organization. Numerous studies have suggested that organizational constraints and demands represent a major source of stress and burnout (Drory & Shamir, 1988; Leiter & Maslach, 1988; Maslach & Jackson, 1984; O'Driscoll & Schubert, 1988; & Pines & Aronson, 1988).

Organizational Change

Cherniss (1995) suggests seven implications for organization policy and practice. The first is increased attention to caregiver impact when planning new programs. She suggests an impact study before a new program is fully operational to understand how the changes will influence providers' work environments, non-professional duties, types of clients to be seen, variety and change, and allowances for individual differences. Second, burnout could be reduced if administrators encouraged providers to develop special-interest programs. Encouraging creativity and flexibility again enhances self-efficacy. Some professionals will need little more than explicit permission for such activities, while others might need more direct administrative support. Third, agencies should provide sensitive and supportive supervision to providers that are working with difficult clients. These sessions must not be punitive; rather, they should serve as an opportunity to deal with psychological reactions to difficult clients and to develop realistic expectations.

Another important area for training is organizational negotiation skills. The most effective providers know how to work the system. They are able to effect organizational change while giving attention to both efficiency and compassion. Similarly, when an outside expert suggests change, staff that will be potentially affected by such recommendations must be part of the planning from the beginning and must be allowed to make the ultimate decision as to what changes are implemented.

Finally, Cherniss (1995) suggests that all other things being equal, it is wise to hire staff who have successful previous work experience and provide ongoing career counseling and professional development. Flett, Biggs, and Alpass (1995) emphasize coping strategies, organizational factors, social support, management skills and knowledge, and education and training.

Workplace consultant Beverly Potter (Rohlk, 1998) notes that a major cause of burnout is feelings of helplessness and powerlessness. Workers are happier when they have room to grow in a job and are not hampered by bureaucracy, an overcritical boss, or office politics. Similar to previous writers, Potter suggests four strategies for employee empowerment: 1) setting goals that are specific, achievable, observable, and measurable; 2) encouraging participation and fostering trusting communication; 3) providing feedback that is constructive and goal-oriented; and 4) acknowledging performance in a timely manner and for small achievements as well as larger ones.

LOOKING AHEAD

Clearly, burnout is a serious threat to worker morale and ultimately to organizational effectiveness, yet it continues to run rampant in many social-service agencies. The encouraging news is that there are specific and achievable strategies that can stop burnout. Some of the most promising strategies require pervasive organizational change (in which we are most interested). As we will show in later chapters, person-centered organizational leadership and management, a particular form of participatory management, can be quite effective in controlling burnout and its negative effects on personnel, clients, and the agency. Unfortunately, this phenomenon is prevalent in nonprofit organizations at the beginning of this 21st century. Yet, its reduction or elimination can provide the key to empowering social-service personnel to work on a more predictable basis and to perform social-service miracles like the one that Jason, our poet, needs so desperately.

DEBATE: TRANSFER OF METHODS FROM PROFIT TO NONPROFIT SETTINGS

The potentials within participatory management models for increasing quality of service, decreasing professional burnout, and creating longer-term effects on fiscal responsibility and community betterment seem impressive when one considers the way in which these models work within many parts of the for-profit sector. Yet, is it possible for a top-notch service agency to be run in the same way as a top-notch corporate organization? If so, is this situation desirable? Valid distinctions exist between these two types of organizations. The presence or absence of a profit motive and use of volunteer personnel constitute critical differences that, for some, create the conclusion that any transfer of management methods from one to the other type of organization is inappropriate. Before arriving at our own point of view of this fundamental issue, we look to the history of nonprofit management in this country.

Evolution of Social-Service Management

Ramanathan and Hegstad (1982) point out that if the *New York Stock Exchange* (NYSE) had listed nonprofit organizations, they would have been considered the growth industry of the 1970s. Such a view is more valid than exaggerated. Prior to that decade, social-service activity was largely administered by large, centralized organizations such as welfare departments (DuBois, 1981). Following the social awakenings of the 1960s was the realization that government alone was not the sole solution to society's less fortunate. Tens of thousands of small, community-based, nonprofit agencies and programs were created across the country to meet these needs at the grass-roots level (Clifton & Dahms, 1993). Accompanying this growth in nonprofit services and the number of agencies was also a growing concern about the value of socially useful services obtained for every dollar spent. Scarce resources, competition from other nonprofit organizations, and changing public attitudes began to exert pressure for nonprofit accountability (Clifton & Dahms, 1982; & Toch & Grant, 1982).

Writers argued, however, that the adoption of management techniques from the for-profit sector was inappropriate. Lack of a profit motive (Ramanathan & Hegstad, 1982), larger involvement of non-agency persons (DuBois, 1981; & White, 1981), and rampant worker burnout (Toch & Grant, 1982) have all been cited as critical distinctions between these two types of organizations. Further exacerbating the problem was the shortage of academic programs specifically designed to prepare managers for work in not-for-profit organizations (Clifton & Dahms, 1993). Administrators were often former service providers who gained managerial skills on the job. This transition was not, however, necessarily seen as positive. Lewis and Lewis (1983) summarized this situation succinctly:

> Human service professionals used to cringe when they heard the term management. That word raised, for many, the specter of the pencil-pushing bureaucrat—surrounded by paper and cut off from the lifeblood of day-to-day work with clients. Unfortunately, this stereotype led many human service deliverers to avoid becoming competent in management for fear that they might somehow be turning their backs on their clients or losing their professional identification as helpers (p. 1).

We suggest that the perceived chasm between the managerial needs and skills required in nonprofit and for-profit organizations is inflated, if not artificial—especially if the newer corporate-participatory management models are the focus of attention. (For cutting-edge approaches that are not necessarily oriented toward participatory management, refer to Barbeito & Bowman, 1998; Bernstein, 1997; Carver, 1997; Charan, 1998; Frantzreb, 1997; Hamilton & Tragert, 1998; Herman & Heimovics, 1991; Letts, Ryan, & Grossman, 1999; & Steckel & Lehman, 1997.)

A Useful Approach to the Issue

We should note the reality that most of the commentators in this area have been thinking about older management models as they reached the conclusions that they have popularized. Thus, traditional wisdom in the nonprofit field has held that for-profit methods could result in the debasement of goals and missions if imported for use in social-service settings. Yet, the corporate-management methods to which these writers refer are conventional, decidedly not participatory in philosophy and strategy. Participatory management methods shift the focus from profit to quality and from artificial incentives to genuine interest in worker well-being. Be it product service, profitable service, or nonprofit service, it might be that this participatory management philosophy leads to effective outcomes despite the organization's raison d'être. Given the importance of the nonprofit mission and the intriguing successes and possibilities associated with participatory management, a variety of nonprofit organizations now look forward to investigating the possibilities. A person-centered participatory management approach, such as that detailed in this book, might prove to be effective in reducing burnout in a variety of social-service settings. But, before we look at this unique, American approach to participatory management, we must give some general attention to the potentials that are inherent in participatory management models and the successes and failures reported to this point.

REFERENCES

Banaszak-Holl, J. and Hines, M. A. (1996). Factors associated with nursing home staff turnover. *The Gerontologist*, Volume 36, pp. 512–520.

Bandura, A. (1977). Self-efficacy: Toward a unifying theory of behavioral change. *Psychological Review*, Volume 84, pp. 191–215.

Bandura, A. (1982). Self-efficacy mechanism in human agency. *American Psychologist*, Volume 37, pp. 122–147.

Barbeito, C. L. and Bowman, J. P. (1998). *Nonprofit compensation and benefits practices.* New York: John Wiley & Sons, Inc.

Barrett, K., Riggar, T. F., Flowers, C. R., Crimando, W., and Bailey, T. (1997). The turnover dilemma: A disease with solutions. *Journal of Rehabilitation,* Volume 63, pp. 36–44.

Barrett, K., Crimando, W., and Riggar, T. F. (1993). Becoming an empowering organization: Strategies for implementation. *Journal of Rehabilitation Administration,* Volume 17, pp. 159–167.

Bernstein, P. (1997). *Best practices of effective nonprofit organizations.* New York: The Foundation Center.

Carver, J. and Carver, M. M. (1997). *Reinventing your board: A step-by-step guide to implementing policy governance.* San Francisco: Jossey-Bass.

Charan, R. (1998). *Boards at work: How corporate boards create competitive advantage.* San Francisco: Jossey-Bass.

Cherniss, C. (1993). Role of professional self-efficacy in the etiology and amelioration of burnout. In W. B. Schaufeli, C. Maslach, and T. Marek, eds., *Professional Burnout: Recent Developments in Theory and Research,* pp. 135–149. Washington, D.C.: Taylor and Francis.

Cherniss, C. (1995). *Beyond burnout: Helping teachers, nurses, therapists, and lawyers recover from stress and disillusionment.* New York: Routledge.

Clifton, R. L. and Dahms, A. M. (1993). *Grassroots organizations: A resource book for directors, staff, and volunteers of small, community-based, nonprofit agencies* (2nd ed.). Prospect Heights, IL: Waveland Press.

Dignam, J. T. and West, S. G. (1988). Social support in the workplace: Tests of six theoretical models. *American Journal of Community Psychology,* Volume 16, pp. 701–724.

Drory, A. and Shamir, B. (1988). Effects of organizational and life variables on job satisfaction and burnout. *Group & Organization Studies,* Volume 13, pp. 441–455.

DuBois, P. M. (1981). *Modern administrative practices in human services.* Springfield, IL: Charles C. Thomas.

Firth, H. and Britton, P. (1989). Burnout, absence and turnover amongst British nursing staff. *Journal of Occupational Psychology,* Volume 62, pp. 55–60.

Flett, R., Biggs, H., and Alpass, F. (1995). Job stress and professional practice: Implications for rehabilitation educators. *Rehabilitation Education,* Volume 9, pp. 275–291.

Frantzreb, A. C. (1997). *Not on this board you don't: Making your trustees more effective.* Chicago: Bonus Books.

Freudenberger, H. J. (1974). Staff burnout. *Journal of Social Issues,* Volume 30, pp. 159–165.

Freudenberger, H. J. (1975). The staff burnout syndrome in alternative institutions. *Psychotherapy: Theory, Research & Practice,* Volume 12, pp. 72–83.

Geurts, S., Schaufeli, W., and DeJonge, J. (1998). Burnout and intention to leave among mental health-care professionals: A social psychological approach. *Journal of Social and Clinical Psychology*, Volume 17, pp. 341–362.

Golembiewski, R. T., Munzenrider, R., and Carter, D. (1983). Phases of progressive burnout and their work site covariants: Critical issues in OD research and praxis. *The Journal of Applied Behavioral Science*, Volume 19, pp. 461–481.

Hamilton, L. and Tragert, R. (1998). *100 best nonprofits to work for: Find your dream job and launch a rewarding career doing good!* New York: Beach Brook Productions.

Herman, R. D. and Heimovics, R. D. (1991). *Executive leadership in nonprofit organizations*. San Francisco: Jossey-Bass.

Jackson, S. E., Schwab, R. L., and Schuler, R. S. (1986). Toward an understanding of the burnout phenomenon. *Journal of Applied Psychology*, Volume 71, pp. 630–640.

Jevne, R. F. and Williams, D. R. (1998). *When dreams don't work: Professional caregivers and burnout*. Amityville, NY: Baywood.

Krakinowski, L. (1992). Preventing burnout. *Rehabilitation Today*, Volume 2, pp. 18–23.

Leiter, M. P. and Maslach, C. (1988). The impact of interpersonal environment on burnout and organizational commitment. *Journal of Organizational Behavior*, Volume 9, pp. 297–308.

Letts, C. W., Ryan, W. P., and Grossman, A. (1999). *High performance nonprofit organizations: Managing upstream for greater impact*. New York: John Wiley & Sons, Inc.

Lewis, J. A. and Lewis, M. D. (1983). *Management of human service programs*. Monterey, CA: Brooks/Cole.

Maslach, C. (1976). Burned-out. *Human Behavior*, Volume 5, pp. 16–22.

Maslach, C. (1993). Burnout: A multidimensional perspective. In W. B. Schaufeli, C. Maslach, and T. Marek (eds.), *Professional burnout: Recent developments in theory and research*, pp. 19–32. Washington, D.C.: Taylor and Francis.

Maslach, C. and Jackson, S. E. (1984). Patterns of burnout among a national sample of public contact workers. *Journal of Health & Human Resources Administration*, Volume 7, pp. 189–212.

Maslach, C. and Leiter, M. P. (1997). *The truth about burnout: How organizations cause personal stress and what to do about it*. San Francisco: Jossey-Bass.

Mirvis, D. M., Graney, M. J., and Osborne-Kilpatrick, A. (1999). Trends in burnout and related measures of organizational stress among leaders of Department of Veterans Affairs Medical Centers. *Journal of Healthcare Management*, Volume 44, pp. 353–365.

O'Driscoll, M. P. and Schubert, T. (1988). Organizational climate and burnout in a New Zealand social-service agency. *Work and Stress*, Volume 2, pp. 372–204.

Pines, A. and Aronson, E. (1988). *Career burnout: Causes and cures*. New York: Free Press.

Ramanathan, K. V. and Hegstad, L. P. (1982). *Readings in management control in nonprofit organizations*. New York: John Wiley & Sons, Inc.

Riggar, T. F., Barrett, K. E., and Crimando, W. (1995). Applied discipline. *Journal of Rehabilitation Administration*, Volume 19, pp. 89–101.

Rohlk, L. (1998). Beating job burnout. *Incentive*, Volume 172, pp. 121–123.

Steckel, R. and Lehman, J. (1997). *In search of America's best nonprofits*. San Francisco: Jossey-Bass.

Stevens, P. (1995). *Beating job burnout: How to turn your work into your passion.* Lincolnwood, IL: VGM Career Horizons.

Toch, H. and Grant, J. D. (1982). *Reforming human services: Change through participation.* Beverly Hills: Sage Publications, Inc.

Wade, D. C., Cooley, E., and Savicki, V. (1986). A longitudinal study of burnout. *Children & Youth Services Review*, Volume 8, pp. 161–173.

White, S. L. (1981). *Managing health and human services programs*. New York: Free Press.

2

Possibilities in Participatory Management

PARTICIPATORY MANAGEMENT AND BURNOUT

One of us recently talked with a woman named Beth, a middle manager in a New England firm that has had person-centered leadership in place for so long now that many associates pretty much take this system for granted. In an arrangement brokered by senior executives, she had been loaned to a client organization for a few months because of some specific skills that were needed in that location. She said that the client company's product line fascinated her, but she found the entire 10-week experience mostly distasteful. While the company has a fairly good reputation as an employer that pays good wages, gives great benefits, and promotes good people quickly, the company is structured along the lines of traditional management models. Decisions and information travel downward within the organization. Little communication exists among departments, and there is a noticeable amount of competition among them. Conventional suggestion boxes are liberally scattered throughout the organization's four floors of corporate offices. Beth said that to her, those suggestion boxes "said it all." They were a constant reminder that the voices of those who were lower in the organization could not be routinely heard. Top management did not understand that suggestions, comments, and every other form of employee input ought to (and can) flow freely within the normal channels of communication. "When you've got a system that needs to rely on a special box in order to get associate suggestions, you've got trouble! Besides," she said emphatically, "nobody puts real suggestions in those boxes anyway! I'll bet there's a connection between suggestion boxes and good management. Wherever you find those boxes, you can bet you won't find great management!"

Although we are unaware of such a study, our guess is that Beth is right about the suggestion box. In participatory-management organizations, good ideas tend to bubble up rather than filter down. Importantly, comments and suggestions are easily passed along through normal communications channels. These suggestions are at the heart of what continuous quality improvement is all about (Snyder, Dowd, & Houghton, 1994; & Quinn & Spreitzer, 1997). This improvement requires listening and requires management to pay attention to the real experts—the men and women who are out there doing the work.

So, what does all of this information have to do with nonprofit management? The answer is, "Possibly everything." When you have a social-service role in your job, you are particularly likely to need to be heard. When your job is to have an impact on problems such as those that we talked about in the previous chapter, you are especially vulnerable to the attitudes and policies of your organizational-management structure. When the source of salaries is voluntary public giving, we can find management trying to play it as safe as possible, encouraging the conservative and being wary of the obviously creative.

Yet, nonprofit employees are in special need of backup systems that support and enhance front-line efforts. They need their most exciting, yet perhaps most unconventional ideas to be taken seriously at the home office. They need to know that somebody will sit down with them to provide encouragement for their frustrations, praise for their successes, common sense and a little wisdom for their confusions, and understanding for their failures. A leadership and management team approach that involves this sort of input and support can get hard jobs done.

Heretofore in management history, however, perhaps the most important element that nonprofit employees need has been hard to come by and sometimes even harder to articulate. *Long before burnout ever becomes a significant personal issue, nonprofit workers need to be able to turn to a system that can help them meet the unique emotional and practical needs that this kind of career provokes.* When faced on a daily basis with client poverty, disease, disability, lack of education, crime, violence, and often really rotten interpersonal skills, the social-service worker needs to be part of an especially effective team—a team that includes everybody from the finance officer to the office secretary.

When faced on a daily basis with insurmountable odds and almost unbelievable expectations, a nonprofit associate needs also to be faced daily with dozens of large and small organizational factors that compensate and make it possible to effectively cope. When a nonprofit associate receives this kind of support, significant amounts of burnout can be prevented. This kind of organizational structure is a solid response to the factors that can lead to burnout (many of which we mentioned in Chapter 1, "Survival within Today's Nonprofit Organizations: Pressures and Burnout.")

In this book, while we present a case study of an organization that uses a specific sort of participatory management, person-centered leadership, these strategies can only be understood once a clearer picture emerges of just what participatory management in general is all about. After we consider the important differences between leadership and management, the remainder of this chapter is devoted to a discussion of the participatory-management phenomenon.

LEADERSHIP AND MANAGEMENT: CRUCIAL DIFFERENCES

Sometimes, the terms *leadership* and *management* have been used interchangeably as if they referred to the same expectations and similar sets of strategies and responsibilities. A standard dictionary tells us that "to lead" means "to guide or show the way; to bring by reason, cogency, or other influence to some conclusion or condition." The same source states that "to manage" means "to control and direct; to bring about by contriving; to supervise and administer." While we begin to get a feel for the differences between these definitions, we cannot infer from them the sharp distinctions that are needed if we are to make sense of the issues. Thus, we start to understand why there has been some confusion regarding these constructs. Fortunately, the organization literature has struggled with the problem, and useful insights are emerging.

Management

A leading management textbook of the 1980s presents a definition of management that represents a common understanding. This basic definition of management was popular and prevalent throughout the latter half of the

20th century and continues to work well. Management refers to "the attainment of organizational goals in an effective and efficient manner through planning, organizing, and controlling organizational resources" (Daft, 1988, p. 755). Unlike the case with leadership definitions, this basic sort of management definition has not been seriously questioned, although a variety of management philosophies with dissimilar-sounding titles have been in use. For example, *management by objective* (c.f., Odiorne, 1978) and *management by walking around* (Peters & Austin, 1985) have gained popularity as behavioral-management terms. In the former approach, a manager uses the attainment of objectives as a sort of performance appraisal, while in the latter approach, managers seek direct conversation with personnel in order to exchange information. While the title and strategies suggest that there might be mutually exclusive philosophical differences between the two strategies, in fact, finding managers who practice both sets of strategies is not uncommon. We often find the two approaches compatible methodologically, given conventional management goals. We mention these two management strategies here for the sole purpose of illustrating that most management strategies, although disparate, are used to accomplish the fundamental goals identified in the preceding definition. A good manager is expected to control and allocate resources, including knowledge, supplies, and finances, in order to effectively and efficiently plan and organize on behalf of the company's mission and goals. A good manager is expected to understand the organization's master plan and how his or her department's functions fit within the process. The manager is charged with interpreting this plan to those who work within that designated unit. Ultimately, the manager is responsible for the unit's production.

The same popular late-1980s management textbook defines the term leadership as "the ability to influence other people toward the attainment of organizational goals" (Daft, 1988, p. 755). This meaning clearly reveals the existing confusion, because the definition reads as if it, too could represent an adequate definition of the term *management*. We can find little fundamental difference between the definitions of the two terms. We are of the opinion that the confusion over the management versus leadership concepts during the last part of the previous century reveals an embedded conviction of that time that the most primary characteristic of good organizations is that they are the result of good management—at the top and at the middle ranks. Probably, it is fortunate that the strength of this point of view is on the decline. Leadership and management are different phenomena, but they are both crucial for organizational success.

Leadership

As global competition and communication have become the norm, organizational theorists (Clark & Clark, 1990; Kotter, 1996; & Podsakoff, MacKenzie, Ahearne, & Bommer, 1995) have developed an even deeper respect for the role of organizational leadership. With this respect has come a more careful definition of the term. Management schools and texts have begun to emphasize even more the development of leadership skills in addition to managerial skills.

Many have noted that a multiplicity of leadership definitions exists. At times, it might appear as if no two are quite in agreement (Stogdill, 1974; & Yukl, 1998). Some years ago, Katz and Kahn (1978) noted that whatever leadership is, it clearly is something more than the ability to achieve compliance with "routine directives of the organization." A basic and often-cited definition of leadership produced by John Gardner (1990) holds that "leadership is the process of persuasion or example by which an individual (or leadership team) induces a group to pursue objectives held by the leader or shared by the leader and his or her followers" (p. 1).

We believe that inherent within that oft-quoted definition is the simple but powerful meaning of the term that has been attributed to former U.S. President Dwight D. Eisenhower: "Leadership is the ability to know what needs to be done and the ability to influence others to do it." By extension, leadership is all about vision and inspiration. Indeed, Kouzes and Posner (1996) concluded that an effective leader is both visionary and practical, inspires through both example and words, fosters shared values, takes immediate action, and possesses credibility and character.

Distinctions

Understanding the differences between management and leadership is becoming increasingly important, and we must not use the terms as if they were redundant. A good leader provides vision and inspiration to the organization. A good manager plans, mobilizes, and guides in support of organizational needs and goals. Given these distinctions, a leader quite possibly does not need to necessarily manage, and a manager does not necessarily need to lead.

Nanus and Dobbs (1999) recognize the distinctions that we have drawn. When writing about nonprofit leadership, they make several key points. They stipulate that responsibilities are different between managers and leaders, as are the bases upon which the two groups are evaluated. Yukl (1998) says that while it might be useful to distinguish between the processes of management and leadership, it might not be appropriate to label people as exclusively one or the other. Indeed, because a variety of occupational titles incorporate the term "manager," they reason that it would be insensitive to insist that only those who have been hired to be leaders can lead and that those who are hired to manage should develop only managerial functions.

The Yukl position seems most useful for our discussion. No matter what role a person occupies within an organization, leadership occurs when he or she is developing (or helping to develop) new goals—new visions supported by inspiration. Conversely, when an individual is strategically, routinely, or creatively implementing the vision, plans, and goals of others, management is in progress. Throughout the discussions that follow, you will find that we do not use these terms interchangeably. When we talk about leadership, at the core of the conversation is our recognition of the leadership components of vision and inspiration. When we talk about management, we are concerned with functions such as planning, guiding, developing, and facilitating. The definitions of person-centered leadership and person-centered management that appear in the next chapter are unique to those particular forms; nonetheless, you will find the differences to be compatible with the general distinctions drawn here.

PARTICIPATORY MANAGEMENT: HISTORY AND SUCCESSES

A discussion of participatory-management models best begins within the context of a discussion of the differences between leadership and management. Given that this movement has been called "participatory management," does it follow that these models are oriented away from organizational leadership and toward organizational administration that is bereft of vision and inspiration functions? The answer is, "Certainly not." In fact, quite the opposite is true. The fact that the genre has been most often referred to through the use of the term "management" is an historical accident. As we will see, participatory management emerged in the mid-20th century as a response to faltering traditional models of organizational structure and leadership. Because the management concept was the one most in vogue and most in use in organizations during the latter part of the previous century, those who experimented with the newer participatory strategies quite understandably thought of them as management derivatives. Fairly quickly, people clearly saw that leadership was a core component of these participatory models. At that point, however, the term "participatory management" was so widely in use that it remained the descriptor of this set of models. Nonetheless, wherever you encounter this term, you should remain somewhat cautious. Only by pursuing an understanding of the context within which the term "participatory management" is used can the reader grasp whether leadership or management is the actual topic of discussion. In this book, we typically use the conventional term "participatory management." Nonetheless, we recognize that most of the participatory models emphasize leadership as well as management functions. We encourage you to adopt a similar understanding of the term as you move through the chapters of this book.

History of the Models

The story of the beginnings of the participatory-management movement has been told often. The original visions are most often attributed to W. Edwards Deming, an American who, shortly after World War II, managed to get the attention of Japanese corporate leaders at the same time he was failing to get the attention of U.S. corporate executives (Killian, 1992; Latzko, 1995; Neave, 1990; & Walton, 1986). His message was basic and reasonably easy to comprehend. He said that it was bad practice to develop quality-assurance programs wherein companies guaranteed that if a product did not work, they would replace the product. Rather, he said, a company should make sure that it does not make any defective products in the first place. He talked about quality improvement, rather than quality assurance. All processes should be continually subjected to careful review and retooling in order to constantly improve every aspect of design, production, and marketing, he believed. Adages such as, "If it ain't broke, don't fix it" represented the major impediment to quality. Leaders were encouraged to replace these attitudes with a philosophy of continual improvement. Even the best and most popular of products were to undergo constant scrutiny and development.

Manufacturers were told that problem products resulted from problem systems, not problem workers. They were to get rid of the system glitches that resulted in poor products, but how? Deming supported the use of a 14-point program that called for graphing processes statistically and driving fear out of the organization. Basically, his message was clear: pay attention to the front-line worker. That person is your expert and knows the real causes of defective products and system inefficiencies. In other words, get the executives to work for the laborers, not the other way around.

In Japan, this kind of message was culturally consistent with a mainstream Japanese perspective (DeMente, 1981). Despite failures in other parts of the world, the design and manufacturing successes of Japanese companies became almost legendary at one point. No matter where a corporation was located, however, in order to implement a Deming-based strategy, companies had to involve the worker in key management decisions. Rather quickly, the idea of participatory management began to take hold internationally. Today, a huge percentage of profit-making companies all over the globe have tried some form of participatory management. In fact, because spectacular early failures were reported (c.f., Brown, Hitchcock, & Willard, 1994) as well as spectacular successes, we must note that the movement has gone through several changes and cycles just during the past 25 years. Repeated attempts to produce participatory-management models that work well and reliably in this country have begun to bear great fruit (for example, Lancaster, 1999; & Tichy, 1997). Finding a company that has not been affected by these management ideas in some way is difficult these days, because many companies have committed to exclusive use of these strategies.

Typical Participatory-Management Strategies

We must realize that there are probably as many participatory-management strategies and models as there are organizations that use them. This movement has developed in several directions—some of them rather distinct from one another (for example, Block, 1993; Bolman & Deal, 1995; Briskin, 1998; DePree, 1992; & Senge, 1990). Even a highly touted successful model, such as the one in place at General Electric (Slater, 1999), has not seemed to take root in a variety of locations. Rather, versions of participatory management abound. Common strategies exist that most models endorse, however.

People pay a lot of attention to *systems thinking* in these models. When something goes wrong, everyone starts looking for a glitch in a system process. Associates are careful not to blame an individual at these moments, because they assume that more trouble is caused by ineffective policies and procedures than is caused by ineffective workers.

Continuous quality improvement becomes a mission for the company. All departments are challenged to continually rethink the way they do things—

goals, designs, processes, procedures, output, and communication. No matter how well a given procedure might be working, the procedure is always subject to re-evaluation. The goal is to create processes that result in only quality products. Defective products of any sort are not acceptable, no matter how few might be produced.

Rather than expecting people to learn all that is needed in order to fulfill their job functions, management expects that it has hired a *learning workforce*. This workforce understands the necessity to continually learn new skills and adopt new perspectives in this ever-changing world of the 21st century. No one is expected to know everything, but everyone is expected to know how to learn what is needed in order to work smartly in any given situation.

A commitment to employee *empowerment* exists (Cotton, 1993). In other words, management attempts to make it easy for employees to make decisions and to help create company commitments and directions. Each employee—regardless of his or her role in the company—is expected to be the expert at his or her job and is treated accordingly. Management does not try to second-guess worker judgements and decisions. Senior executives and middle managers tend to believe that one of their important functions is to meet the needs of those who actually design, produce, and market the product.

In general, in successful participatory-management environments, you are likely to find associates who feel more respected than those who are managed in more conventional ways. You will see that workers at every level tend to be more initiating. They seek out new responsibilities and solutions to new and old problems, and they tend to feel rewarded for their efforts. Less blame exists. The typical worker knows something about the workings of other departments as well as the company budget. Less information is held secret by top management. Those who are lower on the pay scale tend to be more honest about their evaluations of the company and tend to feel that they are part of the big picture. In a well-run participatory-management organization, you are likely to find a majority of people telling you that they truly like working for the organization and believe that they are respected and valued by those in management and executive positions.

The Individual

The emphasis on treating the individual as an expert and empowering him or her to make decisions on behalf of the company is one of the most powerful and intriguing aspects of these newer management models. In fact, this aspect might be the most important fundamentally. Early on, the U.S. corporate sector—like other developing corporate sectors in other countries—created a reputation for itself as being an uncaring place within which to work (Bass, 1985; & Rayback, 1959). Too many corporate "yes men" and executives who drove their people to exhaustion negatively colored our attitudes about the possibilities in corporate environments. A large percentage of Americans developed the belief that corporate environments were insensitive, uncaring, and simply out to make a buck at the expense of the worker and even the customer, if necessary (Brooks, 1964; & Dubofsky, 1985). Thus, the history of how the corporate world began to return attention to the individual, to turn the corner toward a more compassionate and socially responsible future, is of some interest as well as importance (McGregor, 1960; Pfeffer, 1998; & Tom, 1997). In the United States, the roots of the relevant changes can be found in psychology as well as in organizational literature and experience.

Psychological Roots

Kurt Lewin (1935; & Marrow, 1969) was one of psychology's most popular early teachers and researchers. His work and that of his colleagues (Lewin, Lippit, & White, 1939) provided the insights that stimulated modern research on motivation. During World War II, while studying the influences that prompted people to buy the kinds of foods that they do, Lewin and his coworkers realized that group dynamics can be influential in forming attitudes. He also discovered that front-line individuals, such as housewives, are often the source of the most critical decision-making for the group.

Tjosvold and Tjosvold (1995) provided a comprehensive overview of the psychological themes within the leadership literature. The early influential work produced by Bass (1960, & 1985)—a long-time, leading organizational psychologist—examined what happens when workers do not think they are respected or heard. He showed that effective managers know how to understand what their workers need and want. They know how to act on that knowledge in a way that inspires productivity and trust. Social psychologists Emery and Trist (1969, & 1972) also have studied the responses of individuals to particular management strategies. For example, they have shown that great teamwork is associated with the personal satisfaction of individuals. Many other psychologists have looked at things such as self-determination (Klein, 1987), self-esteem (Brown & Smart, 1991), and feelings (Plas & Hoover-Dempsey, 1988) as they have tried to understand what motivates working people to do good work and what contributes to their senses of well-being while on the job.

Perhaps the most important contribution to the foundations of participatory management and person-centered leadership, however, was made by the eminent psychotherapist Carl Rogers (Rogers, 1986; & Seeman, 1990). His primary method of psychotherapy was basically a simple one. He trained psychologists to listen—deeply listen—to what the client was saying. He called his method *person-centered psychotherapy*, because he wanted the psychologist to remain continually and intensely focused on what the client was truly expressing and feeling. This approach to therapy is intellectually quite similar to many participatory-management strategies, especially person-centered models. These therapists expect to find that individuals have important understandings about their problems. The client, like the worker, is presumed to have all of the expertise that is necessary in order to get the important work done.

Organizations and the History of Worker Participation

In most areas of the world (and in most business-related fields), the beginning of the participatory-management movement occurred sometime between the 1930s and 1950s, resulting in the landmark thinking of W. Edwards Deming (introduced previously). By the 1970s, as early Japanese manufacturing successes captured the rest of the world's attention, *quality circles*, an approach based on Japanese Deming-style management, started to crop up all over the world (McGill, 1988). Within a group discussion format, key people would confront company issues, problems, and visions of the future. As the name implies, the continual development of quality processes and products was the main thrust. Yet, people dealt directly with issues of morale during these meetings, because it was understood that if workers were unhappy, quality would necessarily suffer. Despite so much early interest in quality circles, the rest of the world soon discovered that it could not simply institute quality circles and hope to achieve the kind of outstanding results in quality manufacturing that the Japanese were experiencing routinely (Levine, 1995). A mindset and business that was different from that understood in the West clearly permeated Japanese culture. As DeMente (1981), Durlbahji and Marks (1993), and others point out, the typical Japanese person culturally comes to understand that the group or team—a collection of people working together—is the source of all good things that have ever been envisioned or produced by human beings. In the

United States, for example, the culture suggests that all good things envisioned or produced have resulted from the efforts of an individual—the sacred individual who ultimately is responsible for his or her actions, be they contributory or non-productive. This sort of difference in perspective represents what caused many of the earlier quality circle and other participatory-management efforts to fail in this country as often as they did (Howe, Gaedert, & Howe, 1995; & Jacob, 1994). As theorists, researchers, and company executives began to analyze the failures, quite a few U.S. companies started to figure out how to make at least some components of the quality improvement models pay off. Most important among these was the emphasis on getting workers to participate in management decisions and implementations (Cotton, 1993; Gitlow, 1995; & McLagan & Nel, 1995).

For the past 20 years, finding an issue of a creditable business periodical that does not contain an article presenting some aspect of the participatory-management phenomenon is nearly impossible, and books describing the philosophy abound (c.f., Crosby, 1999; Maister, 1997; & Bradford & Cohen, 1998). Top-down, authoritarian ways of running corporate organizations seem to have cycled through their strongest moment of influence. They have given way to those models that focus on team-based initiatives and employee empowerment. A proliferation of these newer methods has surfaced, and most companies—large and small—have incorporated at least some participatory-management and leadership strategies.

IN CONCLUSION

Following 80 to 100 years of experience with industrialization, participatory management emerged on the world stage as a response to the production of goods and services of poor quality, and worker dissatisfaction had been targeted as contributing to this state of affairs. Organizational theorists searched for the most crucial factor in the production process and found it in the individual worker. They reasoned that the front-line employee understood what worked and did not work in that unit and was likely the only person who knew where the real problems resided. They also believed that the front-line employee had a sufficient grasp of the situation to know how to fix problems and to prevent them before they occurred. A philosophy of management developed from this point of view and spawned an assortment of participatory models. A variety of components aimed at developing the voice of the worker included treating the employee as an expert, establishing meaningful work teams, driving fear out of the organization, and creating work environments for lifelong learning. These approaches have met with varying levels of success, depending on such things as the national and organizational cultures in which they root, the visioning capabilities of the leadership in place at the time, and the ability of managers to understand and endorse the basic principles.

A difference exists between organizational leadership and management. Both are completely crucial if an organization is to succeed. Leadership results from vision and inspiration; management requires planning, facilitating, and strategic skills. Many individuals in today's organizations are hired into managerial positions where these latter skill sets are mandated. Yet, those who are in these managerial positions can quite possibly exercise leadership authority as they develop new visions and inspire employees. Conversely, an individual who is hired to provide leadership functions for the organization can demonstrate managerial skills as he or she works on follow-through and implementation.

To the extent that managers empower employees to assist with vision spinning and peer encouragement, they function as participatory managers. Likewise, when those who are in leadership positions encourage others to imagine and create the organization's future, they act within a participatory-management model.

Referring to participatory models as participatory management has been conventional within the literature. In actuality, most such models have heavy leadership components built in at all parts of the process and throughout the infrastructure. Throughout the remainder of our discussions of the issues, we will adhere to the convention of referring to these models as participatory management, except where we are intent on reminding the reader that the idea of leadership is fundamentally important to the discussion. We hope you will consistently think of both leadership and management functions when you encounter the participatory-management term within the remaining chapters.

REFERENCES

Bass, B. (1960). *Leadership, psychology, and organizational behavior.* New York: Harper & Row.

Bass, B. (1985). *Leadership and performance beyond expectations.* New York: Free Press.

Bass, B. (1985). *People, work, and organizations.* New York: Allyn & Bacon.

Block, P. (1993). *Stewardship*. San Francisco: Berrett-Koehler.

Bolman, L. and Deal, T. (1995). *Leading with soul*. San Francisco: Jossey-Bass.

Bradford, D. I. and Cohen, A. R. (1998). *Power up*. New York: Wiley.

Briskin, A. (1998). *The stirring of soul in the workplace*. San Francisco: Berrett-Koehler.

Brooks, T. R. (1964). *Toil and trouble: A history of American labor*. New York: Delacorte.

Brown, J. D. and Smart, S. A. (1991). The self and social conduct: Linking self-representations to prosocial behavior. *Journal of Personality and Social Psychology*, Volume 60(3), pp. 368–375.

Brown, M., Hitchcock, D., and Willard, M. (1994). *Why TQM fails*. Burr Ridge, IL: Irwin.

Clark, K. E. and Clark, M. B. (eds.). (1990). *Measures of leadership*. West Orange, NJ: Leadership Library of America.

Cotton, J. L. (1993). *Employee involvement*. Newbury Park, CA: Sage Publications, Inc.

Crosby, P. B. (1999). *Quality and me*. San Francisco: Jossey Bass.

Daft, R. L. (1988). *Management*. Chicago: Dryden Press.

DeMente, B. (1981). *The Japanese way of doing business*. Englewood Cliffs, N.J.: Prentice Hall.

DePree, M. (1992). *Leadership jazz*. NY: Dell.

Dubofsky, M. (1985). *Industrialism and the American worker* (2nd ed.). Arlington Heights, IL: H. Davidson.

Durlbahji, S. and Marks, N. E. (1993). *Japanese business: Cultural perspectives*. Albany: State University of New York (SUNY) Press.

Emery, F. and Trist, E. (1969). *Form and content in industrial democracy: Some experiences from Norway and other European countries*. London: Tavistock.

Emery, F. and Trist, E. (1972). *Toward a social ecology: Contextual appreciations of the future in the present*. London: Plenum.

Garner, J. (1990). *On leadership*. New York: Free Press.

Gitlow, H. (1995). *TQM in action*. New York: Prentice Hall.

Howe, R., Gaedert, D., and Howe, M. (1995). *Quality on trial* (2nd ed.). New York: McGraw-Hill.

Jacob, R. (1994). TQM: More than a dying fad? *Fortune*, Volume 128(9), pp. 66–72.

Katz, D. and Kahn, R. L. (1978). *The social psychology of organizations* (2nd ed.). New York: John Wiley & Sons, Inc.

Killian, C. S. (1992). *The world of W. Edwards Deming* (2nd ed.). Knoxville: SPC Press.

Klein, J. (1987). Employee stock ownership and employee attitudes: A test of three models. *Journal of Applied Psychology*, Volume 72, pp. 319–332.

Kotter, J. P. (1996). *Leading change*. Cambridge, MA: Harvard Business School Press.

Kouzes, J. M. and Posner, B. Z. (1996). Seven lessons for leading the voyage to the future. In F. Hesselbein, M. Goldsmith, and R. Beckhard (eds.), *The Leader of the Future: New Visions, Strategies, and Practices for the Next Era*. San Francisco: Jossey-Bass.

Lancaster, H. (August 31, 1999). Herb Kelleher has one main strategy: Treat employees well. *Wall Street Journal.*

Latzko, W. J. and Saunders, D. M. (1995). *Four days with Dr. Deming.* Reading, MA: Addison Wesley.

Levine, D. I. (1995). *Reinventing the workplace: How business and employees can both win.* Washington, D.C.: Brookings Institute.

Lewin, K. (1935). *A dynamic theory of personality.* (K. E. Zaner and D. K. Adams, trans.). New York: McGraw-Hill.

Lewin, K., Lippit, R., and White, R. (1939). Patterns of aggressive behavior in experimentally created social climates. *Journal of Social Psychology,* Volume 10, pp. 271–299.

Maister, D. (1997). *True professionalism: The courage to care about your people, your clients, your career.* New York: Free Press.

Marrow, A. J. (1969). *The practical theorist: The life and work of Kurt Lewin.* New York: Basic Books.

McGill, M. E. (1988). *American business and the quick fix.* New York: Holt.

McGregor, D. (1960). *The human side of enterprise.* New York: McGraw-Hill.

McGregor, D. (1965). *Leadership and motivation.* Boston: *Massachusetts Institute of Technology* (MIT) Press.

McLagan, P. and Nel, C. (1995). *The age of participation.* San Francisco: Berrett-Koehler.

Nanus, B. and Dobbs, S. M. (1999). *Leaders who make a difference.* San Francisco: Jossey-Bass.

Neave, H. R. (1990). *The Deming dimension.* Knoxville: SPC Press.

Odiome, G. S. (October 1978). MBO: A backward glance. *Business Horizons,* pp. 14–24.

Peters, T. and Austin, N. (1985). *A passion for excellence: The leadership difference.* New York: Random House.

Pfeffer, J. (1998). *The human equation.* Cambridge, MA: Harvard Business School Press.

Plas, J. M. and Hoover-Dempsey, K. V. (1988). *Working up a storm: Anger, anxiety, joy and tears on the job.* New York: Norton.

Podsakoff, P. M., MacKenzie, S. B., Ahearne, M., and Bommer, W. H. (1995). Searching for a needle in a haystack: Trying to identify the illusive moderators of leadership behaviors. *Journal of Management,* Volume 21, pp. 423–470.

Quinn, R. E. and Spreitzer, G. M. (1997). The road to empowerment: Seven questions every leader should consider. *Organizational Dynamics,* Volume 26(2), pp. 111–121.

Rayback, J. G. (1959). *A history of American labor.* New York: MacMillan.

Rogers, C. P. (1986). Reflections of feelings. *Person-Centered Review,* Volume 1, pp. 375–387.

Seeman, J. (1990). Theory as autobiography: The development of Carl Rogers. *Person-Centered Review,* Volume 5(4), pp. 373–386.

Senge, P. (1990). *The fifth discipline: The art and practice of the learning organization.* New York: Doubleday.

Slater, R. (1999). *The GE way fieldbook*. New York: McGraw-Hill.

Snyder, N., Dowd, J., and Houghton, D. (1994). *Vision, values, and courage: Leadership for quality management*. New York: Free Press.

Stogdill, R. M. (1974). *Handbook of literature: A survey of the literature*. New York: Free Press.

Tichy, N. M. (1997). *The leadership engine: How winning companies build leaders at every level*. New York: Harper Business.

Tjosvold, D. and Tjosvold, M. (1995). *Psychology for leaders*. New York: John Wiley & Sons, Inc.

Tom, M. (ed.). (1997). *The soul of business*. Carlsbad, CA: Hay House.

Walton, M. (1986). *The Deming management method*. New York: Dodd, Mead.

Yukl, G. (1998). *Leadership in organizations* (4th ed.). Upper Saddle River, NJ: Prentice Hall.

3

Person-Centered Leadership

Person-centered leadership is a unique form of participatory management that directs as much attention to the individual as to the team, requires senior leadership to be responsible for empowering people at all levels of the organization, and develops quality through continuous attention to organizational culture and system processes (c.f., Arnold & Plas, 1993; Briskin, 1998; Pfeffer, 1998; & Plas, 1996). Person-centered leadership tends to operate somewhat differently from organization to organization because its successful execution depends upon the specific individuals who implement it and the unique culture in which it is developed. If person-centered leadership is a special form of participatory management, however, what are its unique features? How does this approach differ from other participatory models? Why might this management be the best choice for nonprofit organizations?

A PRIMARY DISTINCTION BETWEEN PERSON-CENTERED LEADERSHIP AND OTHER PARTICIPATORY-MANAGEMENT MODELS

Western countries, particularly the United States, have a history of culturally and legally focusing on the rights and responsibilities of the individual. Person-centered leadership is uniquely suited to U.S. and other Western organizations, because it recognizes the cultural primacy of the individual. Unlike many other participatory-management models, in a person-centered organization, attention to the team is not considered more important than attention to individual effort and well-being. This distinction is critical, and understanding this concept is crucial for recognizing the potentials that are inherent in the person-centered leadership model.

TEAMWORK AND THE NEW MANAGEMENT MODELS

As organizations in many countries began to test Japanese quality-improvement methods in Western settings, it certainly seemed that effective teamwork was at the core of the Japanese management project. Manufacturing settings in Japan used a team approach as the vehicle for getting upstream, continuous improvement into their processes. Certainly, focus on the individual was important, because real expertise was thought to reside in individual workers. Observers tended to believe that teamwork was the vehicle for change, however. A within-unit group approach and cross-departmental liaisons seemed to introduce quality into the enterprise. So, many organizations in other countries enthusiastically endorsed teamwork as the most exciting management innovation of the '70s, '80s, or '90s, depending on which decade was hosting all of the experimentation. In retrospect, it is a little surprising to realize that the failures of new management in westernized countries (Jacob, 1994; & Nohria & Berkley, 1994) that kept appearing were rarely thought to be the product of misguided attempts to develop dependence on teamwork strategies. People blamed many other factors (Howe, Gaedert, & Howe, 1995), but rarely did an observer locate the source of the problem in cultural issues of individualism versus the team. Nonetheless, it now seems that this factor might have been critical. In the United States, we tend to believe that we are a country of teamwork players and that the addition of strong teamwork to the corporate agenda should come easily and result in quick successes. Despite the mountains of literature on the cultural importance of American rugged individualism that has been produced from the days of Alexis de Tocqueville (1969) forward, it was not until relatively recently that some (Kotter, 1995; Plas, 1996; & Schrage, 1995) began to speculate that failures might have resulted at least partially from a clash of cultural values—from a confusion over how to develop teamwork without sacrificing individuality. While many participatory-management strategies have recognized the importance of the individual's expertise for the company, they have tended to give greater focus to the development of teamwork strategies and team rewards.

Person-centered leadership is completely compatible with this country's emphasis on the sacredness of the individual. These management strategies give as much attention to the development of the individual as they do to the development of team functioning. In fact, some person-centered for-profit organizations pay as much attention to the worker's needs as they do the customer's needs (for example, Rosenbluth, 1992). Others endorse the assumption that neither constituency should be primary. All might agree that ultimately, the worker's interests, company's interests, and the customer's interests clearly should be the same. The way to make the customer happy is to make sure that the worker is happy. The message is simple, yet powerful—especially within countries that value the rights and roles of the individual as much as the United States does.

THE ROLE OF THE INDIVIDUAL IN U.S. CULTURE

One almost perfect spring afternoon, I ran into a for-profit health-care middle manager of my acquaintance at a central park area in the city where I live. His spirits did not seem to match the day, and I inquired further. He complained that his current company was so intent on "this teamwork thing" that it was "throwing the baby out with the bath water." When I asked him what he meant, he said that his unit had quotas to fill by the end of the fiscal year and that "they're tying our hands because they say we've got to produce, but they won't let us alone to do what needs to be done. They keep insisting that a few of our guys work with some of the people in Accounts Receivable. They say they want a 'team approach' to this thing. But, I ask you, isn't it my ass that's going to be on the line when it all goes belly up? No *team* is going to get the blame!"

Unfortunately, this man's frustrations and attitudes toward teamwork are not at all unusual across a wide variety of organizational settings. You can find them almost anywhere. When U.S. businesses first became intrigued with the idea of participatory management, the development of an emphasis on teamwork sounded great. In fact, this approach almost sounded easy. But once corporations gained experience with participatory-management models, lots of folks found team membership to be confusing, frustrating, and even threatening. Many people also found it boring. Hearing complaints that teams never get anything done, take forever to make the smallest decision, and are usually burdened by at least one goof-off is not uncommon. The truth seems to be that most Americans do not adapt easily to a team approach at work at the same time that most Americans think people here are naturally good at it. This apparent contradiction needs close scrutiny as the country moves into the 21th century, where teams will be located at the center of an organization's communication, production, and evaluation systems. Teamwork is probably here to stay, and we need to get better at it.

The Individual's Primacy

As they reflected on American identity, Bellah and his associates (1985) wrote the following:

> We believe in the dignity, indeed the sacredness of the individual. Anything that would violate our right to think for ourselves, judge for ourselves, make our own decisions, live our lives as we see fit, is not only morally wrong, it is sacrilegious. Our highest and noblest aspirations, not only for ourselves, for those we care about, for our society and for our world, are closely linked to our individualism. (p. 142)

People here are taught the value of thinking for themselves and making their own decisions. They are expected to take responsibility for their actions, whether things turn out beautifully or badly. Unlike many other countries, our legal codes are based on the rights of the individual as well as on the potential culpability of the individual. You and your friends are expected to "pull yourselves up by your bootstraps," and you have been taught that the buck always stops at an individual's desk.

As we noted previously, in other countries such as Japan, people have grown up believing that anything great that has ever been achieved was ultimately the product of a group effort. Americans have grown up believing that anything great that has ever been achieved was originally the product of an individual effort—of a single person's heroic vision.

A country that has so consistently revered individual effort cannot expect its citizens to instantly embrace a new philosophy of organizational teamwork. A culture that has rewarded and punished the individual cannot be expected to quickly adopt a work ethic that locates responsibility within a group. Certainly, within organizations, these things cannot be reasonably expected in the absence of training programs that teach employees how to bridge the gap between individualist expectations and teamwork strategies.

Teamwork

Despite our historical focus on rugged individualism, we still seem to think of ourselves as team players. Early in the history of participatory management, most executives assumed that team strategies would be among the easiest parts of the model to develop. This situation was not so, however. Larson and LaFasto (1989), an academic and corporate executive, respectively, studied the problem of team effort and reported the following:

> We seem to lack the essential ability to work together effectively to solve critical problems. In fact, the potential for collective problem solving is so often unrealized and the promise of collective achievement so often unfulfilled that we exhibit what seems to be a developmental disability in the area of social competence. The potential is there. The realization of that potential too often is not. (p. 13)

Sports Teams   The best example we have of effective teamwork here are our sports teams. Obviously to most players, coaches, and fans, the talented teams who work together best are the ones who score the most points. When the team does not work well together—during a single game or during the whole season—the lack of teamwork is painfully obvious to everyone.

Two factors are responsible for athletic teamwork success in the United States (Plas, 1996): role differentiation and individual recognition. The people on the team need to know what their roles are and how a role fits with everyone else's responsibilities. The importance of the second factor, recognition for individuals, is less obvious and only critical in countries such as the United States that have an individualist ethic. Here, an individual expects to receive recognition for a job well done.

Work Teams   While not too many people experience the roar of the crowd when they are put into the game, most people frequently do experience (or at least expect) some form of "atta boy" when they get the job done. In environments where that sort of positive reinforcement is missing, people tend to work less hard, complain more, and report reduced levels of job satisfaction (George & Brief, 1992; Levine, 1995; & Schrage, 1995). When teamwork is emphasized to the exclusion of individual recognition, some Americans do not know how to function well, others do not want to, and far less creativity is expended in service of the project or company.

Therefore, the point is that nonprofit groups that want to use participatory-management strategies are well-advised to use a method, such as a person-centered approach, that enables people to get their individualist cultural expectations met and that teaches them how to develop strong teams that can produce what is needed. The organization that you will learn about in the following chapters has become adept at meeting needs for individual recognition and being fundamentally team based. This sort of participatory management is needed if nonprofit organizational issues such as burnout are to be responded to with any hope of successful outcome.

HOW DOES A UNIQUE PERSON-CENTERED MODEL OPERATE?

In a good-sized, family owned company in the Midwest, an executive vice president in charge of operations schedules two hours every Monday morning for keeping tabs on his regional manager. He does not do what you might expect during these phone conversations, however. He always begins the talk by saying, "What do you need from me this week?" His intention is to serve, rather than direct. He wants to know what the particular manager needs in order to develop his or her department—and equally important, he wants to know what assistance he can provide that would enhance the manager's personal development projects. A high level of trust exists between this vice president and the people with whom he works. He cares about them as much as he cares about the company's market position and profit margins. This situation does not, of course, mean that he likes all of his managers in the way that he likes his friends. This situation does mean, however, that he is committed to their development as people and as professionals. That was not always how things were conducted. For the first three years of his work with this company, he and others in the organization played by the old rules that they had all picked up in their *Master of Business Administration* (MBA) programs some 20 years ago. Without giving it much thought, they had operated by using conventional organizational wisdom that said you would be successful if you did the following:

- Always play things close to the chest
- Never let them see you sweat
- Understand that there can be only one chief
- Make it a habit to be hard to find

There were some good, experienced, bright people running this company, so some wondered why it only had a modest profit margin and why employee turnover was one-and-a-half times the national average for the field. The inescapable conclusion was that management models and strategies were outdated and ineffective. The owners hired consultant help. Changing the leadership system became job one.

After a few years of working hard to transform the company from a top-down bureaucratic organization into a person-centered leadership system, people at all levels of this company have come to believe that the new methods are for real and that they are here to stay. The transition was never easy, however. As this particular vice president put it, "changing the way this company relates to its employees was probably the hardest thing I've ever been part of—but maybe the most rewarding."

Person-centered leadership is a type of participatory management that pays as much attention to employee development as company development. In fact, it is presumed that these components are one and the same. Kerm Campbell, as chief executive officer of Herman Miller, articulated well the prime principle of person-centered leadership and management:

> We've got to help people build lives as well as careers. We start with the employee, because I believe that you have to get it right inside before you can do it right outside. My focus is on liberating the human spirit within the company, so we can furnish environments to our customers that will allow them to reach their full potential. (Day, 1994, pp. 38-39)

DePree (1992) says,

> Delegation requires that leaders adopt certain goals, goals that require us to think of achievement as a collaborative and synthetic result. We need both efficiency and effectiveness. Personal development and growth must accompany meeting the organization's needs. (p. 156)

What we hear in both sets of remarks is a new kind of organizational thinking: a person-centered approach to the business of business.

BASIC PRINCIPLES

Within a person-centered model, it is important to *empower* the worker to make decisions, provide vision, and take action. Gone are the days of having to ask for permission to think and create and having to submit a simple request in triplicate. Yet, person-centered leadership is much more than just a simple empowerment strategy. This approach is based on a philosophy that says the worker is not only capable, but also valuable. Employees are as important as the products and customers.

In person-centered organizational environments, a continual shift of focus exists from individual to team and back again. *Teamwork* matters a great deal. People are encouraged to pool their strengths and to compensate for one another's weaknesses. Inter-departmental rivalries and hostilities are forcefully discouraged. Often, the organization sees itself as a *learning environment*. Employees believe that working smartly means knowing how to solve problems and where to go to find the information needed. People do not believe that an accumulation of facts will ensure success, because important and relevant facts can change. Rather, workers adopt a career-long commitment to education. *Risk-taking* is an important and accepted strategy, as well. Employees learn to take informed risks on behalf of the organization, client, and their own personal and professional development. *Inverted organization charts* guide communication and decision making. Executives and managers know that the front-line worker makes or breaks the company and that senior leaders are there to serve. Theirs is a facilitative role, rather than a dictatorial role. Naturally, adoption of these sorts of person-centered strategies leads to a *commitment to quality* (Ishikawa, 1986; & Kastner, 1994). This commitment is not reserved just for the product or service, however. Employees also work to develop a quality organization and personal and professional lives that live up to achievable standards of excellence.

The principles and strategies we just described, in various combinations and with various levels of emphasis, can be found within most participatory-management models. The major difference between person-centered leadership and other forms of participatory management centers on a final point: *development of the employee.* The growth and well-being of those who work for the organization takes center stage along with quality, clients, and customers. When this unique, person-centered emphasis is in place, the principles and strategies identified previously are implemented in unique ways. They become something different than when they are used in the absence of deliberate emphasis on the individual.

PERSON-CENTERED LEADERSHIP
AND SERVANT LEADERSHIP

The distinction between person-centered and servant leadership is worth comment. We have noted an important difference.

As envisioned and described by Greenleaf (1996, & 1998), servant leadership has gained a sizable amount of attention from people in organizational America. From his position at the *Massachusetts Institute of Technology* (MIT) Sloan School of Management and the Harvard Business School, Greenleaf launched what some have thought to be a radical revision of the role of the institution in the world. Basic to his vision is the statement that "I believe that caring for persons, the more able and the less able serving each other, is what makes a good society" (1998, p. 5). He has written about the need for new leadership and a new group of men and women who run institutions with listening, empathy, healing, foresight, commitment to the growth of people, and community. Certainly, these are skills that are quite compatible with the philosophy that is found within a person-centered approach to leadership, management, and empowerment. The goals, focus, and emphasis of these two leadership approaches are different, however.

Greenleaf is interested in transforming the world stage and changing society. He writes about religious leaders as easily as he writes about corporate executives. He talks about universities as often as he talks about governments. Greenleaf wishes to impart wisdom to a world that has lost touch with the values that birthed it. Thus, we see Greenleaf wanting to transform the university, seminary, corporation, and political environment. He calls on leaders to serve, and he believes that servant leadership will result in the creation of institutions that challenge and inspire human beings to develop at faster rates toward a more wholesome and honest future.

Servant leadership is often thought of as a movement. Person-centered management is an organizational-leadership approach. The goal of person-centered leadership is far more particular than that of the servant-leadership movement. True, some person-centered leaders care about the transformation of society. The typical person-centered leader is intent on developing a way of making it possible for empowerment and participatory models to actually work within organizations that operate within an individualist culture, however. Where teamwork makes sense—and yet, does not work— person-centered leadership philosophy and strategies can make a crucial difference in the success of participatory initiatives.

Thus, it seems to us that the philosophy and values that are inherent within a servant-leadership approach to the future are compatible with person-centered organizational leadership. What person-centered leadership provides that is missing in most servant-leadership discussions, however, is careful attention to the cultural reality of individualism. This leadership model seeks to maintain the value of individualism while simultaneously engendering new appreciation and dependence upon teamwork, collective work, and decision making.

Person-centered leadership suggests that the individual employee should be as important to the organization as the organization's fundamental mission, be that profit or nonprofit. This philosophy is certainly reminiscent of a servant-leadership ethic. Person-centered leaders have tended to desire a two-fold result from the establishment of a person-centered model, however: the organization's responsibility to the individual who contributes to it, and a vastly improved quality of the product, service, and customer/client relationships.

Clearly, these two approaches to leadership have much in common. The basic difference results from a difference in emphasis: society versus participatory organizations and how to get them to work, and the world stage versus specific individualist cultures. No doubt, the successful implementation of both approaches results in a better-prepared citizenry and brighter future for the children of those who labor in today's world.

PERSON-CENTERED LEADERSHIP VERSUS PERSON-CENTERED MANAGEMENT

An emphasis on individual employee development and empowerment means that leadership functions emerge throughout the organization. When the personal and professional growth of the employee becomes a goal of the organization, that employee is necessarily exposed to opportunities for leadership development. Associates at all levels of the company are encouraged to use vision and inspiration and major leadership functions as they work within teams to accomplish quality work. So, when person-centered leadership is in place, the management model in that organization becomes (almost by default) a leadership model. Certainly, management functions such as planning, guiding, and developing continue to be required by the organization. What is also then required, however, is employees expecting themselves to engage in leadership functions in addition to appropriate management functions.

THE IMPORTANCE OF UNIQUENESS

All person-centered organizations, whether corporate or nonprofit, fold in the principles and strategies we just described. Each accomplishes this task in a notably unique way, however, because each setting depends upon the talent, vision, and interests that exist within the particular people who comprise the organization at a given time. The development of the individual means that the uniqueness of individuals begins to carry a lot of weight. The organization grows in ways that reflect the skills and assets of its employees.

No two person-centered organizations are alike in daily operations. The only true similarity resides in a shared commitment to the individual, the team, and the development of quality. Oasis Center, the nonprofit organization that merits detailed attention in the remainder of this book, provides an excellent example of the possibilities for nonprofit leadership and management that are inherent in this emerging leadership model. While the Oasis approach is a good example of person-centered leadership in action, this approach should not be thought of as the only valid approach to a person-centered nonprofit model—because each successful attempt will be unique.

REFERENCES

Arnold, W. W. and Plas, J. M. (1993). *The human touch: Today's most unusual program for productivity and profit*. New York: John Wiley & Sons, Inc.

Bellah, R. N., Madsen, R., Sullivan, W., Swindler, A., and Tipton, S. (1985). *Habits of the heart: Individualism and commitment in American life*. New York: Harper & Row Perennial.

Briskin, A. (1998). *The stirring of soul in the workplace*. San Francisco: Berrett-Koehler.

Day, C. R. (November 7, 1994). Kerm Campbell: We need to change the meaning of management. *Industry Week*, pp. 36–40.

DePree, M. (1992). *Leadership jazz*. New York: Dell.

George, J. M. and Brief, A. P. (1992). Feeling good-doing good: A conceptual analysis of the mood at work—organizational spontaneity relationship. *Psychological Bulletin*, Volume 112, pp. 310–329.

Greenleaf, R. K. (1996). *On becoming a servant leader*. San Francisco: Jossey-Bass.

Greenleaf, R. K. (1998). *The power of servant leadership*. San Francisco: Berrett-Kohler.

Howe, R. J., Gaedert, D., and Howe, M. A. (1995). *Quality on trial* (2nd ed.). New York: McGraw-Hill.

Ishikawa, K. (1986). *Guide to quality control* (2nd ed.). Tokyo: Asian Productivity Organization.

Jacob, R. (1994). TQM: More than a dying fad? *Fortune*, Volume 128(9), pp. 66–72.

Kastner, R. (1994). *The ISO 9000 answer book*. New York: John Wiley & Sons, Inc.

Kotter, J. P. (1995). *The new rules*. New York: Free Press.

Larson, C. E. and LaFasto, F. M. J. (1989). *Teamwork: What must go right, what can go wrong*. Beverly Hills: Sage Publications, Inc.

Levine, D. I. (1995). *Reinventing the workplace: How business and employees can both win*. Washington, D.C.: Brookings Institute.

Nohria, N. and Berkley, J. (January-February 1994). Whatever happened to the take-charge manager? *Harvard Business Review*, pp. 128–137.

Pfeffer, J. (1998). *The human equation*. Cambridge: Harvard Business School Press.

Plas, J. M. (1996). *Person-centered leadership: An American approach to participatory management*. Thousand Oaks, CA: Sage Publications, Inc.

Rosenbluth, H. F. and McFerrin Peters, D. (1992). *The customer comes second*. New York: Quill, William Morrow.

Schrage, M. (1995). *No more teams*. New York: Doubleday.

Tocqueville, A. de. (1969). *Democracy in America*. (G. Lawrence, ed.: J. P. Mayer, trans.). New York: Doubleday Anchor. (Original work published in 1835.)

PART **II**

A PERSON-CENTERED, NONPROFIT EXAMPLE OF EXCELLENCE

INTRODUCTION

In a person-centered, nonprofit organization, leadership and management must do everything possible to help workers effectively cope with their feelings and barriers that exist—their personal pain and red tape. This job is management's No. 1 task, and a person-centered leadership team knows that fact. By extension, the arguably radical (but nonetheless fundamental) fact of person-centered, nonprofit leadership is: The *main function of the organizational structure is to serve the employees. The associates serve the needs of the clients, but the organization serves the needs of the associates.*

The Oasis Center, the exemplary agency that we describe in the following chapters, creates client miracles. Actually, Oasis Center associates really would not phrase the statement that way. They would rather say that they empower clients to change their lives. No matter the perspective that one chooses to describe what this center does, however, the basic point is that Oasis gets results. Oasis gets the hard jobs done because it has a stellar leadership and management organizational structure in place that pays as much attention to the employee as it does to the client. In the following chapters, we report some of the major achievements of this agency as we describe in detail the person-centered management model and strategies that the center uses and credits.

The following chapter introduces the agency and furnishes statistics about resources, programs, and client results that you can use to form a more specific idea of the type of agency that we are profiling. Chapter 5, "The Oasis Person-Centered Model," presents the Oasis Center interpretation of a person-centered leadership model. Here, we illustrate specific dynamics, processes, and outcomes in order to give you a feel for how this agency performs its person-centered business.

We must report what works and what does not, how the center's current leadership model helps, and the ways in which this model does not contribute. Thus, we have devoted Chapter 6, "Strengths and Weaknesses: Growing Pains and Growing Satisfactions," to a candid discussion of the Oasis model's strengths and weaknesses.

In Chapter 7, "The Board of Directors: The Creation of a New Participatory Model," we tell you about the unique ways in which the Oasis board of directors functions as we point out specific person-centered strategies that board and staff members have used as they forged their exemplary working relationships. In order to acquaint the reader with Oasis daily functioning, we included Chapters 8 and 9, which describe two aspects of the agency's infrastructure: the shelter and the team-based management component. In Chapter 10, "The Future of Nonprofit Participatory Management," we think about the implications of this person-centered nonprofit case study.

At strategic points within Part Two, we provide strategy boxes that present Bridges to Practice. These specific ideas reflect successful person-centered approaches that associates at Oasis Center have developed and refined. We present them for the reader who is interested in making the transition from theory to practice, from the written word to the practical application.

Throughout the following chapters, we encourage the reader to remember that the Oasis person-centered model is but one way of operating a participatory social-service agency that intends to focus on employees as well as on clients. The uniqueness of each person-centered organization is derived from one of the goals of this sort of management: the development of the individuals who comprise the organization. Thus, we should expect that each organization will create its own model with a philosophy and set of strategies that are compatible with the particular personnel who compose the model. As we will see in the following pages, one of the challenges of person-centered leadership and management is the continual demand for the model to be recreated as former associates move on and new ones join the ranks.

4

Oasis Center
An Overview

This chapter reveals the core of the Oasis Center—the infrastructure, programs, and outcomes of the organization. These components are the nuts and bolts that will introduce the reader to the center. Subsequent chapters provide a richer description of this agency and its strengths and weaknesses. The descriptions and data in this chapter provide the reader with a benchmark for gauging an organization's similarity to the one in this study (Letts, Ryan, & Grossman, 1999).

OASIS: A CENTER OF ACHIEVEMENT

Oasis Center is a nationally acclaimed nonprofit agency that provides comprehensive programs that meet the needs of youth and their families in and around Nashville, Tennessee. On many occasions, the Center has received coveted recognition such as the J.C. Penney Golden Rule Awards and awards from the National Conference for Community and Justice. Oasis has been awarded numerous national demonstration projects by the Department of Health and Human Services. Often, the agency is showcased by groups such as the National Conference for Independent Living, which recently highlighted Oasis programs as the model for best practices in the area. We mention this latter event because, as is so typical with this outstanding organization, when asked to provide a keynote speaker for that conference, they asked one of their teen-aged clients to provide the address. The young woman described struggles and successes in a most genuine and heartfelt way, and by all accounts there was not a dry eye in the house—nor a single audience member who was not impressed by the possibilities. Indeed, any nonprofit organization in the country would be extremely proud to enjoy the Oasis reputation and success rate. This organization is worth emulating.

Oasis is a youth service organization. The center has a program for almost any problem or pressure that a teen-ager might face during the maturing process—crises of alienation, abuse, crime, shelter, and identity. The center's approach routinely puts families, schools, Juvenile Justice, places of worship, and neighborhood groups near the center of the client plan. Most youth who experience the Oasis approach—no matter how hardened or emotionally distant they might be—eventually turn their lives around. The families of Oasis youth clients tend to do the same.

Those last two sentences might be simple statements of fact, but people who are associated with social-service work realize that if they truly *are* facts, the results on which the statements are based must be truly amazing. Despite the complexity and depth of pain driving Oasis client issues and crises, the staff manages to find a way. The credit, they say, needs to be given to their unique person-centered approach to agency and caseload management. They say that they accomplish the impossible or improbable because they run their agency the way they hope their clients can learn to run their families and lives. This agency has adopted some of the newer approaches to person-centered leadership while creating other person-centered strategies that are particularly suited for nonprofit work. Despite the enormous difficulties associated with helping people find their own way out of a crisis, at Oasis, these management strategies are helping get the improbable jobs done.

THE LOCATION

Oasis Center is located on Music Row in Nashville, a modern-day boom town that bills itself as Music City, U.S.A. The center is currently housed in a rather modern-looking two-story building purchased three years prior to the beginning of our research project. Before that, Oasis programs were scattered across multiple locations in the city. The building acquisition represented both a symbolic and real coming together of staff and programs. At one time, a small structure next door was leased from a board member to house the shelter program for youth who need temporary residential care. A capital campaign was already underway to raise funds for the main agency building when fire struck and gutted the shelter (refer to Chapter 8, "The Shelter: Against All Odds"). Fundraising efforts were then shifted to a new shelter building.

The organization's location is somewhat up the street from the center of Music Row action. The building is tucked in among several song publishing and entertainment ventures, as well as a smattering of 1930s bungalows and old four-square houses. Little about the façade of the structure calls attention to what goes on inside. If you were a tourist cruising around Music Row, intent on spotting your favorite country-music star, about the only thing that might catch your eye is the occasional front yard banner or poster that the center erects in order to announce something or to thank somebody. Thanking Nashville for its support is one of the center's favorite pastimes. Among the thousands of community people who actively support Oasis are country-music personalities such as Trisha Yearwood and Alan Jackson and the *National Football League* (NFL) Titans' wide receiver, Chris Sanders. They, like others who invest time and money in Oasis projects, know that the organization's logo tells the truth—Oasis Center: Where Teens Succeed.

THE WORK

Nancy Whitehouse has been a caseworker at Metro Nashville's Juvenile Justice center for a while now, working in the Early Intervention Truancy program. Over the course of her time there, she has become pretty familiar with every agency in town that kids in trouble with the law might connect with as they travel their paths to adulthood. She says that Oasis Center is clearly the best. "They design programs for real people with real problems," she says. "If they don't have a program in place, Oasis will create one." When asked why she relies on Oasis, Nancy starts talking about kids and their families. One story she told us concerned a young male who had been living with his grandmother after Juvenile Justice had transferred custody from his mother to the grandparent. While the arrangement at his grandmother's house seemed a lot more stable to the caseworkers, the youngster wanted to go home. Despite the troubles in his mother's house, that is where he wanted to be. People at Juvenile Justice recognized the boy's pain, but they also recognized the grandmother's fears and the mother's insecurities.

They suspected that the current placement might end in a runaway, but they could not, in good conscience, return the child to a home where the parenting was unreliable and exposed him to unacceptable risks. So, they called Oasis.

Soon, the boy, the mother, and the grandmother were enrolled in one of the marathon retreat weekends that Oasis runs as an intervention tool for families who cannot communicate. By the end of the weekend, the mother had made several critical commitments and had impressed the grandmother enough that she was willing to transfer custody back to the mother. The boy had communicated more with *both* of them during that weekend than he had in months. Within days after the retreat, the Oasis staff had plugged him into an after-school program and had developed a counseling program for the family with a center staff member.

The crisis was resolved. The young man, grandmother, and mother had changed in substantive ways. They had connected with ongoing resources for continued development and support. Initial successes blossomed into long-range, positive changes. Juvenile Justice retreated from the case. Nancy Whitehouse told us that sort of story was commonplace when dealing with Oasis Center. She wishes that "other agencies could see how Oasis does it." She said she would like to "clone" the entire agency and position the clones all over town.

Another Juvenile Justice staff member, Sharon Carter, served as an Oasis intern at one time. "If Oasis lays claims, they're valid claims," says Sharon. She, too, talks about specific kids whose lives were turned around by their involvement at this remarkable agency. She told us that we "couldn't find a more nurturing agency in all of Nashville. They nurture teens. They nurture one another. In fact, they nurture the whole community."

The only significant weakness that either of these Juvenile Justice caseworkers can cite about Oasis is the fact that they do not always have room to plug a troubled teen into a program. While it might take a while to get the center's attention, Nancy says that "once they get the kid, they're excellent." Still, both say that from a juvenile court point of view, the center's biggest weakness is that it is not growing fast enough to meet the community's needs.

At Oasis, the staff acknowledges success stories and praise with a not-surprising mix of pride and humility. Yet, the personality of this organization is not easily characterized. Staff responses to events inside and outside the organization are not always predictable to the outsider. Most people who spend a few hours at Oasis find themselves simply startled. This agency is unique and actually makes a significant difference in the lives of troubled youth and their families. In order to accomplish this goal, they had to learn to be creative and to tell the whole truth, even when it feels uncomfortable. Oasis people live within a complex cultural code, and they certainly do not follow all of the typical rules associated with running a nonprofit agency. Most center workers believe that their person-centered leadership and management structure is responsible for making it possible for good people to get the great results that the city associates with Oasis. We set a task for ourselves of unraveling the complexities of this organization so that you can see what is there, what works, and why it works.

THE PHILOSOPHY, CULTURE, AND INFRASTRUCTURE

If you were to ask an Oasis staff member what the organization's philosophy is, you would likely receive as many answers as people you asked. When Ronnie Steine, the agency's current executive director, is asked that question, he suggests that while all descriptions would be remarkably unique, they would probably all include the idea that Oasis Center "is a participatory structure that centers around teams." Steine, Nashville is Vice-Mayor, became the center's director a few years ago, toward the end of the first phase of the research project that forms the basis for this book. As he talks about his first interview for the position at Oasis, he says, "My take, walking through the door, was that while most people couldn't have defined what a person-centered organization is, they were living it without really knowing that they were doing that."

At Oasis, an organizational culture—not an organizational philosophy—guides action. The center's culture is well defined, often discussed, and open to change. Associates can describe that culture in detailed ways, and although each person and each team might perform that task in a unique way, you are likely to get pretty much the same picture across teams and across center personnel.

The Oasis Center culture has created the management model that is described in detail in the next chapter, so we will not outline the specifics of that culture here. Nonetheless, an important characteristic of the culture that deserves immediate attention is the fact that unlike many other organizational cultures, this culture is often altered through conscious choice. In other words, as the center changes its way of doing business from time to time, it also deliberately changes the mores that guide its action. The strategies used to get this job done are almost as fascinating as they are effective. Before we turn to a discussion of the model in the next chapter, however, we will provide the reader with an overview of the center's infrastructure.

Infrastructure and Programs: Today and Yesterday

The Current Story

As the century turned, Oasis was a 50-member staff divided into eight inter-communicating teams (discussed here in alphabetical order): Board Team; Counseling Team; Educational Services Team; Family Retreat Team; Management Team; Shelter Team; Transitional Living Team; and Support Team.

Board Team

The Board Team consists of approximately 24 community volunteers (the number varies slightly from year to year), recruited primarily by current board members who have staff input. Board members can serve up to three two-year terms, and many remain active for the full six years. Two youth members, selected from the Peer Educator program, also serve on the board with full voting privileges during the school year. Typical of nonprofit boards, primary responsibilities include policy determination, budget approval, fund-raising, and the selection and annual evaluation of the executive director. In Chapter 7, however ("The Board of Directors: The Creation of a New Participatory Model"), communication between the board and staff is not routed exclusively through the executive director. At Oasis, board and staff members work and communicate directly with one another.

Counseling Team

The Counseling Team includes seven trained counselors who see teen-age clients and their families on an as-needed and ongoing basis. Grants and community support fund many of the Oasis services, and counseling is offered on a sliding scale. Referrals might come from parents, the community, Juvenile Justice, or other Oasis teams, and counselors work with these referrals in order to ensure a smooth transition of services as well as coordination of client support.

Educational Services Team

The Educational Services Team provides education for shelter clients (approved by the Metro school system). In other words, teen-agers who are staying at the shelter continue their education within the Oasis environment, and all academic work transfers back to the public schools when the teen-ager re-enters that setting. Once again, the Educational Services Team coordinates with other agency teams to provide appropriate care for each individual client.

Family Retreat Team

Work done by the Family Retreat Team represents an intensive family experience for Juvenile Justice referrals that is focused toward reuniting estranged teen-agers with their parents and extended family members. Clients might be former shelter residents and can be referred to the Counseling Team for continuing support.

Transitional Living Team

The Transitional Living Team coordinates a residential program in which young adults ages 18 to 21 live in a group home, maintain a job, pursue appropriate educational goals, and acquire daily-living skills. Graduates from this program and other teen-agers are placed in independent apartments, while still being supervised by staff associates. Adolescents completing the Transitional Living program consistently find success in forging a new life that is positive and effective. Participants might again be referrals from other programs or from other community services.

Management Team

The Management Team is comprised of the executive and associate executive directors, the business manager, development coordinators, and program directors. This place is where most cross-team information sharing takes place as program directors share team activities and concerns and relay cross-team needs and wants. The Management Team is seen not as the top tier, but as one part of the network of Oasis teams.

Shelter Team

The Shelter Team (refer to Chapter 8) supervises a 24-hour residential crisis-intervention facility that houses adolescents who are in need of relief from home runaway, drug abuse, domestic violence, or other family crises that threaten the safety and health of these individuals. As with the Counseling Team, referrals to the shelter can come from other agency teams, other community agencies, or Juvenile Justice. Often, youth are self-referred through a Safe Place program that Oasis has established throughout the city. Bright yellow Safe Place signs are prominently displayed in selected grocery stores, fast-food restaurants, and gas stations, where store employees have agreed to protect any youth who are seeking assistance and to call Oasis for a free escorted ride to the shelter.

Support Team

The Support Team provides auxiliary services such as telephone responses, materials preparation, and bookkeeping. These busy individuals must interface with other staff on a daily basis and provide the first impression that the public receives of Oasis when contacting the agency.

Programs

The teams are the engines that move forward the variety of programs targeting adolescents wherever they are found—in the center, in the schools, in the home, and on the streets. The following is a sample of outcome statistics from the 1998–1999 fiscal year. They provide a snapshot of Oasis's work:

Crisis Calls   The crisis call line is staffed 24 hours a day, typically by the counselor-on-duty (COD). During weekday afternoons, adolescents can also reach peer educators who can share and discuss on a teen-to-teen level. In this fiscal year, 2,395 calls came through the crisis line. The Peer Educators gave 1,400 hours of volunteer service, both for the crisis line and for other agency activities.

Street Outreach   Routinely, a staff associate forages into the community to seek out adolescents who are in need of assistance and who might not otherwise find this help themselves. This individual frequents the bus station, the downtown service center for the homeless, and Riverfront Park—which hosts events that draw young people. An outreach person also routinely visits bridges and overpasses, where the homeless sometimes reside. Last year, the outreach program assisted 645 youth, either with a referral to other help or with a visit to the shelter for at least a shower and food.

Shelter   The shelter is a residential facility where an adolescent can stay for up to two weeks. The shelter's goal is to keep families intact, so part of the shelter program provides individual, family, and group counseling sessions during a young person's stay. During the reporting period, the Oasis shelter served 208 clients. An overwhelming percentage, 91 percent, did not end up in state custody after shelter residency. They returned to the nuclear family or to another relative. Sixteen percent of these clients were self-referred, which is an indicator that the Safe Place program is working (or at least, that Nashville youth somehow are aware of the Oasis services). In total, the shelter provided 1,099 individual counseling sessions, 327 family counseling sessions, and 1,900 group counseling sessions.

Transitional Living   The Transitional Living program provides a longer-term living arrangement (up to six months), where youth can develop educational, work, and financial goals for independent living. In 1998–1999, Transitional Living served 21 individuals. Forty-three percent of those were self-referred. Again, this number is an indicator that Oasis services are known and used within the local adolescent population. The average length of stay in Transitional Living was 29 days, and 90 percent of program participants successfully moved to independent-living situations.

Outpatient Counseling   The seven counselors on the Counseling Team provide as-needed and ongoing therapy to adolescents and their families. During this most recent reporting year, 18 new clients were served on an individual basis only (in other words, youth only). Furthermore, 73 additional youth were served for whom support to families was also provided. These new clients are in addition to an already-established client base. Ongoing cases included 69 youth-only clients, 258 youth and family clients, and 31 home-based clients who, for a variety of reasons, could not come to the center and were seen in their homes.

School-Based Groups   Groups are held in a variety of schools. These groups include primary prevention work, mother-daughter groups, and other groups. In the reporting year, 325 new clients attended these group sessions.

Family Retreat Weekend   Thirty-five families participated in the Family Retreat Weekend.

PULSE   This innovative community volunteer program has seen, in its second year, 414 youth members working in 189 volunteer projects throughout the Nashville community. They provided 2,406 hours of volunteer service. These statistics represent the month-to-month projects and do not include annual PULSE day statistics, during which there is a concentration of volunteer efforts throughout the community on one Saturday in April.

Alternative Spring Break   In the spirit of volunteerism, Oasis also sponsors an *Alternative Spring Break* (ASB), during which youth and staff associates travel out of town during spring break to provide services to identified needy recipients. In 1998–1999, Oasis sponsored two projects, with 19 youth participants donating 570 volunteer hours.

Teen Outreach Program (TOP)   TOP is a pregnancy-prevention program for adolescents that is provided in the school setting. In addition, participants are invited to give back to the community through a service project. In 1998–1999, 246 youth were involved in the program and participated in 113 community-service projects, totaling 2,560 volunteer hours. These youth-volunteer hours do not overlap with PULSE program volunteers but are in addition to them.

ELECT   The ELECT program targets school dropouts who are in state custody and provides educational services to prepare for the *General Equivalency Diploma* (GED). Seventeen people participated in the ELECT program, with 44 percent passing the GED. Nineteen percent were referred to other educational resources when more help was needed.

Youth Employment   This program provides training and strategies for resumé writing, skills development, and other preparatory training for job readiness. In the reporting year, 124 youth participated in this service.

Funding

The 1999–2000 Oasis budget totaled $1,407,177. The center's funding sources are as follows:

- Federal: Department of Health and Human Services, 36 percent

- State: Department of Health and Department of Children's Services, 28 percent

- Local: Metropolitan Government of Nashville/Davidson County and the Metropolitan Development and Housing Agency: 6 percent

- Other: United Way, 30 percent

History

Oasis began in 1969 as a Rap House response to drug use and demonstrations in the streets of Nashville. Oasis was incorporated in 1970 with a health clinic component and evolved that decade to extend its services to schools and to clearly define its mission to teen services. In the 1980s, Oasis developed fundraising mechanisms and formulated several critical programs, including foster-care services, the Youth Network for Juvenile Justice, Independent Living, Safe Place, ELECT, home-based counseling, and the youth advisory committees. In this closing decade of the 1990s, Oasis has developed the emergency shelter program, sponsored the teen outreach program, and developed the ELECT program. The Family Retreat Weekend was begun, and the new emergency shelter was built.

A PERSPECTIVE ON THE ORGANIZATION'S CORE

What we have just presented is a rather straightforward look at the basics of the Oasis operation—its history, infrastructure, programs, and budget. While these statistics can be useful for an agency that chooses to benchmark itself with the Oasis Center in mind, they do not reveal the most important parts of the agency—and they do not tell the biggest parts of the story.

The center is committed to team-based functioning, maintains a dozen major programs, has successfully competed for national, state, and local grant funding and philanthropic giving, and operates responsibly within a budget of approximately $1.5 million. These realities are impressive; yet, they do not constitute the Oasis core reality: *This organization is as committed to the individual staff member as it is to the team and to the client.* The model described in the following chapters reveals that this agency has a youth-focused mission and that it realizes its targeted goals through the constant re-creation of a dance that first showcases the individual associate, then the team, then swings back toward an individual, and so on. This situation is a never-ending merge of individual and team-based dynamics.

REFERENCE

Letts, C., Ryan, W., & Grossman, A. (1999). *High performance nonprofit organizations: Managing upstream for greater impact.* New York: John Wiley & Sons, Inc.

5

The Oasis
Person-Centered Model

The most fundamental difference between the Oasis Center's approach to participatory management and other participatory-management approaches is possibly the biggest reason for its success. At Oasis, the staff member is as important as the client. This organization is as committed to the development of the center associate as it is to the development of the troubled teen-ager and family who are the objects of organizational commitment. This point should not be under-emphasized, because it so radically departs from traditional management philosophies and from many other participatory models. As you encounter the Oasis person-centered model in the following pages, you will come upon almost countless references to the importance that they place on providing attention and resources to the nonprofit staff member. After moving through a description and analysis of the model, you will find at the end of the chapter a discussion of the formal leadership role in establishing the model some years ago.

THE VALUE OF THE INDIVIDUAL

For-Profit Organizations and the Client

In most traditional management models (Drucker, 1954; and Hoxie, 1918), the product and the company were believed to be the most sacred. Why? The answer is that people reasoned that these components were the constants. Workers, executives, and customers might change, but the company itself was going to be around for quite some time. In the '30s, '40s, and '50s, a company's products were ideally made to last forever—and even the demand for the product was expected to endure. For example, in the late '40s, it simply did not occur to companies, workers, or customers that the market for those metal, spring-back outdoor chairs could disappear as new materials (vinyl), new styles (outdoor chaise lounges), and new needs (stackability and portability) might emerge. As cultures and organizations evolved, however, people around the world began to experience new possibilities and new realities. Companies merged, changed, and went out of business. Market shares and quality characteristics received more and more attention. Expecting that products would become outdated—many of them quite quickly, as in the computer-related businesses—was routine. Thus, a primary focus on the durability of the company and the long-range market for its products gave way to a primary valuing of the customer.

Nonprofit Organizations and the Client

While the durability of the nonprofit agency in the community has always been important, many of these organizations have always paid more attention to the client than to any investment in a specific type of service. In a significant sense, the need for a customer focus has always been a little easier for a service agency to grasp. For this reason, and others, a move toward participatory management, where a customer focus is so important, in some ways can be less problematic for nonprofit organizations.

The Oasis Model and the Individual

As other participatory-management projects work toward putting the customer and client at the focus, however, the Oasis model already goes beyond that. Oasis people take for granted that the primary reason for the agency's existence is to meet a community need by serving the client in outstanding ways. So, they never take their eyes off their client constituency. They have learned, however, that in order to meet the client's needs well, the staff worker's needs also must be met. Perhaps even more importantly, in order for workers to be able to provide growth opportunities for clients, workers have to be given growth opportunities for themselves. If the client is to be treated with dignity, fairness, support, trust, and a positive attitude, then the staff worker has to be treated just as well. While this sort of reasoning makes sense to many, the ways in which Oasis Center has carried this approach into practice have been novel—and ultimately impressive—because of its effectiveness.

THE OASIS MODEL

The Implicit Model Within the Culture

The Oasis organizational culture is, in effect, the organization's policy manual. Little distinction exists between the center's culture and its philosophy and methods of management. Contrast that with most other contemporary organizations—even the good ones—where the philosophy, structure, management methods, and company policies are usually written down, while the company culture, which is not written down, often does not reflect those things but nonetheless guides decision-making and action. For example, it is not uncommon to find a company that says or believes it values teamwork, yet develops a culture that works against teamwork. This situation typically results in inter-departmental rivalries and a lack of cooperation. A belief that "cream always rises to the top" often means that individuals who stand out are rewarded more than others. Those who achieve starring roles will reap rewards, despite an alleged commitment to team efforts.

At Oasis, what you see is what you get. That is, the organizational culture is not separated from philosophy and policies. In fact, if the culture changes in such a way as to propel the need for a new policy, such a policy change is made only after the staff has convinced themselves that a real culture change about the issue has indeed occurred. For example, several years ago, as associates began to understand that they really did want and need to support their own personal lives, several staff members began to suspect that bringing their pets to work for a few days might lessen strains associated with worrying about old and sick dogs and pets. These pets needed temporary care during the day. Some who brought pets, like Denise Becker with her dog Hannah and Rebekah Walker with Mika, began to recognize that having pets around on a full-time basis provided many positives and few negatives. Pets were a great help in coping with the constant high-stress levels, and many clients felt more at ease in the presence of a lovable dog.

Eventually, the issue of bringing pets to work was more or less formally addressed by seeking wisdom within the informal organizational culture. Some offered comments. Others asked for opinions on the subject. Management Team personnel listened and contributed to the center's unique version of a rumor mill in order to get good direction in the matter. In due time, dogs and other pets could be seen on a regular basis around Oasis. Now, if you ask whether a policy about the practice exists, associates would likely tell you the policy in adequate detail, but they would have no idea whether the policy was written down somewhere.

Symbols are important reflections of organizational culture here. Oasis Center's formal symbol of a palm tree in the desert reflects its mission of providing hope and renewal in the otherwise often-parched lives of young people. The informal, seemingly insignificant symbols also tell a story, however. An in-house telephone directory is alphabetized by first names, rather than by last names—reflecting the personal touch that is so important to the culture. The fuchsia-colored questionnaires in the lobby ask visitors and clients to rate the warmth and comfort of the lobby, from reading materials to artwork. During the holidays, displays are rotated to celebrate Hanukkah, Kwanzaa, and Christmas with equal intensity. Native American music was highlighted at the new shelter dedication. These vital symbols reflect the Oasis's cultural commitment to diversity.

So, if you are looking for the Oasis leadership model and its philosophy and practices, you need to look no further than the organizational culture—where the reality of Oasis resides.

The Culture as a Leadership Philosophy and Method

All organizational cultures do not contain the dynamics of the prevailing management model. Indeed, many such cultures arise and are maintained in opposition to the dominant management model.

Within a person-centered model, the organizational culture will likely constitute (de facto) the prevailing leadership and management approach. The reason is because along with the team, individual employees are targeted and individual growth is encouraged—including individual leadership. The particular individuals within the organization develop themselves and develop their management structure. Organizational culture has always resided within the individuals who comprise the group at the given time. When these individuals are responsible for creating their leadership and management strategies, the culture implicitly begins to guide the development and implementation of these strategies in an important way. The Oasis leadership story illustrates this reality quite well. The ways in which these particular dynamics function within this organization become clear throughout this chapter and the following chapters.

The Explicit Model

The Oasis person-centered leadership model rests on a trilateral foundation. Equally basic are the following components: 1) commitment to individual development; 2) empowerment; and 3) team-building. Because the first of these is the most powerful factor discriminating person-centered leadership from other participatory-management models, we begin a description of the Oasis model by looking at the individual focus that permeates this organization's culture.

Commitment to Individual Development

Our research notes reflect our experience that across the life of this study, we never had a single conversation with any Oasis individual or group of individuals that did not contain an important emphasis on the idea that the strength of the center resides in its attitude toward its employees. This commitment to individual development extends to all—those who have secretarial duties and part-time responsibilities, as well as those who are on the Management Team. A point of view exists that is ubiquitous: Oasis cares as much about you, the staff member, as it does about troubled teens and their families. The attitude is realized in many ways, and actions as well as words continually communicate the emphasis. Thus, many identifiable consequences of this management philosophy exist. Among them are the following: personal support, family support, acceptance, and conflict management.

Personal Support

"There isn't any dead wood here," says Sherry Allen, the shelter's director. "Everyone works to sharpen their skills and creativity. We're pacesetters, and it's exciting to be a pacesetter!" Allen is talking about the expectation at Oasis that each associate will contribute in a substantial way to the development of the center's programs and methods. These people are go-getters in all the right ways. They think about community needs and the pains and possibilities that are inherent in the lives of teens who are at risk. They figure out innovative ways to assist, intervene, and stack the decks in favor of kids making good decisions. They do not hesitate to involve the whole family—even several generations of it—and they do not hesitate to get other agencies, companies, and government offices all over town involved in the life of a child. They believe the way to generate creative thinking and problem solving of the caliber that they prize is by provoking and supporting the personal growth of each individual who works at the center. Their person-centered philosophy is simple. You do not have to be a rocket scientist to understand the basic idea: If you are growing and developing as a person and as a professional, so is the agency—and the clients reap the benefits.

Personal Stretches   Frances Rich is on the Shelter Team. "I love this agency," she says. "No place is perfect, but this place is so different from any place I've ever been before." Rich has a reputation around the center for being direct, honest, supportive, reliable, and good to be around. When we asked her just exactly why she loves Oasis so much, the first thing she thought about was the laughter. For her, employee satisfaction manifests itself in the fact that "they work and play well together. The staff has fun." But Rich is talking about something more important than just camaraderie—she is talking about a fundamental organizational approach to personal development. She says that she "used to be afraid to laugh, afraid my laughter would be monitored." But as she and Oasis began to bond, her colleagues encouraged her to develop as a person and as a professional. She realized that they meant it. When she finally began to relax and take advantage of the opportunities here, one of the first areas in which she saw herself changing in a positive direction was in her ability to let the fun out—to generate a good laugh within herself and others.

At Oasis, they are not afraid to laugh or cry. Rebekah Walker, a long-time counselor at the center, used the support of her colleagues to loosen a fear that was preventing her from sharing feelings and tears with her counseling clients. She was trained within a model that insisted that effective counselors would not have feelings about the client's situation, but if they did, they would keep those emotions to themselves. The conventional therapeutic wisdom that she had learned suggests that you would burden a client if you were to let them know what you felt during a session. You would, in effect, unfairly and unprofessionally shift the focus from the client to yourself. Yet, even as a beginning counselor, this approach did not feel quite right to Rebekah. She has always been a strong believer in the power of the relationship to heal. She further thinks that sharing feelings about the client's situation validates the experience of the client and results in an authenticity that provokes trust. At Oasis, she got the support that she needed to begin experimenting with more comfortable approaches to this issue. Her colleagues encouraged her to develop her own style as a counselor and to perfect her craft along lines that took advantage of her strengths. Rebekah says that being with her clients is often a spiritual experience for her as she witnesses the struggles and the odds. She marvels at the ability of the abused and the confused to survive and to prevail. Rebekah connects with her clients who are in pain and who are celebrating. She says that she has learned that sharing her feelings about their struggles and achievements demonstrates the strength of the relationship and the faith that she has in them. When deep feelings arise about a client's experience, she might say, "I need a minute. This is really hard to hear." Or simply, she might say, "I'm so sorry." Other reactions are conveyed by words such as the following:

- I'm honored to be with you.

- I feel better when you come here, too.

- I share your anger at that assault on your precious self. I am outraged.

While this sort of honest emotion—within clear boundaries of a professional relationship—might not be effective for others, Rebekah Walker is known in the community to be a cracker-jack counselor whose clients change in remarkably positive ways. Her personal burnout level is quite low most of the time, partially because her honest feelings about clients are not routinely stifled nor repressed. She credits her current levels of success in this profession to the support that Oasis has given her, and she says that she has come to love her profession with all her heart.

Another counselor, Denise Becker, thinks about the growing center staff and says, "Hardly anyone passes through our doors who does not develop as a person." Yet, as Frances Rich points out, "People are never pushed to do something they're just not ready for." Debra Grimes, the director of administrative services, talks about how the center "places opportunities in front of people—and nobody gets fired if they fail."

Periodically, the teams challenge members to define what they see in their future and to identify the next set of skills that they want to develop. Debra's belief is that "the Oasis people are our greatest strength. They're the biggest asset because they are dedicated to helping others—really committed—at the same time they're dedicated to achieving things for themselves." This thrust is particularly strong and dual for any professional. This approach creates flexibility within an organization as staff members constantly change themselves and become better prepared to cope with the community's changing needs. Issues such as gangs, drugs, and recidivism present increasing challenges to our young people. From a management point of view, this kind of emphasis can almost ensure quality improvement. The people whom you hire this year put newer, even more competent versions of themselves into their positions next year.

A member of the community-based program, Eric Rhinehardt, states that "management treats employees like people they want them to become." Yet, Eric emphasizes that the responsibility is left to the individual, and the hierarchy is not imposed. Eric took a pay cut to come to Oasis from another agency because "Oasis was a better match for me in keeping with my personal values. It has more integrity." He describes Oasis as a safe place to discover for yourself and to ask questions without fear.

THE FAMILY WEEKEND RETREAT   Cheryl Neville and Kelly Falzone present remarkably good examples of the kind of excellence that can occur when talented people are given creative opportunities and substantial amounts of encouragement and support. Both were in their 20s when they developed one of the now most well-known programs at Oasis: the Family Weekend Retreat. They developed this program with Paullette Young (a former center associate) and with the help of their mentor, Denise Becker. We first met with Cheryl and Kelly in a small conference room at Oasis headquarters. While the room was devoid of interesting colors or objects, by the close of the meeting it was full of life, potential, and creative energy. Despite their youth, Becker encouraged these women to develop and execute a challenging and demanding sort of service for families—the kind of program that other sorts of agencies are often unable to advance.

As the 20th century came to a close, Oasis, like other agencies in town, had long felt frustration over the realities of detrimental family influences on teen-agers who were trying to make positive changes. Kids would graduate from social-service programs and Juvenile Justice programs, only to slip back into old habits as they rejoined the family environments that had helped to create those habits. Research showing the important role of family influence on recidivism had become well known here and across the rest of the country. Yet, attempts to involve significant family members in counseling were not paying off. Often, one parent refused to get involved; siblings did not show up; and counselors felt inadequate to convey positive messages in the face of opposing values that were held and voiced by some family members within and outside the counseling session. Too many teens who had sincerely committed themselves to positive changes as a result of voluntary after-school programs and court-ordered program participation succumbed to dysfunctional family dynamics and abandoned those commitments. Other organizations around town, especially Juvenile Justice, had often asked Oasis to develop something that might impact this reality.

In the early '90s, Neville and Falzone were part of the team that decided to put creative energies to work on this problem. They recall that at the beginning, they were completely undaunted by the idea that across the country, few effective programs had ever been created that could make a difference in this often heartbreaking actuality. Their reasons for positive thinking resulted from more than just youth. They had seen other difficult programs developed at Oasis with impressive success. Typical of the Oasis style, Becker encouraged them to develop themselves while they gave this problem a shot. So, they pitched in and helped. At the beginning (and throughout), their three-person team talked through all major issues of process, as well as content. For example, given their experience with the Oasis way of doing things, they realized early on that they needed to talk about their personal styles to make them public and available for feedback. They spent time thinking about intra-team competition and how to make their personal-growth agendas work well together—as a support for the developing program, rather than a hindrance. They planned for communication among themselves about issues of personal style, strengths, weaknesses, and goals, adopting the center's logic that such important factors should not be left to emerge by chance. Falzone says that "Oasis works for me. I feel healthy here and I feel healthy at home because of this." Neville reports that for most of her life, she has been a person who "hates change." But despite her resistance to change, she plunged into this project with the idea that they needed to make their efforts result in a model of flexibility. They clearly pulled that off, and Neville says that one of the consequences has been that she has learned "to get out and do stuff not only for the agency, but also for myself." She speculates that "it's the modeling" that made the biggest difference. Just being around people who push themselves to mature and learn new aspects of personal style has motivated her in her chosen directions.

The program that eventually got off the drawing board and into real life was primarily designed to serve kids who had run afoul of the Juvenile Justice system. Over the years, Juvenile Court—which mandates attendance by teen-agers and their families—has become the primary source of referrals for the program that runs from Friday evening through Sunday, with breaks for families to return to their homes for sleep. The major goal of the Family Weekend Retreat is to create or increase communication within the family. The structures designed to accomplish this goal range from the tried-and-true to the ingenious. Moments of silence, anger, education, games, and high drama exist. The apex of the event is when parents and teens retire to private areas in order to write a letter to one another that is subsequently shared.

As researchers, we participated in one of these weekends. While this book is not the place to describe specific parts of the intervention, it is worth noting that it was obvious throughout the weekend that this experience is the brainchild of people who feel free to create and to innovate in order to accomplish the almost impossible. At the initial Friday-night gathering of adolescents and their family members, we observed largely disengaged young people who made little eye contact and had a downcast demeanor that suggested hopelessness. One hostile young woman—we will call her Kara—spoke vehemently toward her mother in the closing of the session. By Sunday, the close of the retreat, it was amazing to watch the transformation when Kara put her arms around her mother on several occasions and spoke of her hope for a different future. Dramatic change might not occur within each participating family, but it happens often enough to be quite remarkable.

Indeed, the Center and the local juvenile authorities have concluded that a majority of teens and families who attend a Retreat do not reappear on the Juvenile Justice case rolls. Statistics that support this claim are impressive. For example, 100 percent of youth who complete the program are not been placed in a more restrictive environment after one year. In addition, 100 percent of families completing the program and followup session reported no Juvenile Justice charges within the subsequent six months, whereas within a comparable group that did not receive services, 25 percent received new charges.

The retreat methods that these young women devised worked well. Surely, the consistent followup sessions contributes to success. After the weekend retreat, there are three home visits that focus on family goals formulated during the retreat. Referrals are made for additional counseling, if appropriate. A further follow-up occurs three months beyond that, as well.

Falzone and Neville are rightfully proud of what they have accomplished. They are delighted that they are able to make such an important and often life-saving difference in youths' lives. They say that their second-biggest reward is knowing that they were the ones who accomplished this task and that they learned how to achieve at this level of quality and success.

The center is "generous in encouraging autonomy and individuality," says Kelly. "You define yourself as you see fit. For example, I want to use my strengths in my work and one of mine is writing. I've gone on an in-service to learn how to better use my writing at Oasis. Denise's original idea to include letter writing in the Retreat Weekend has proven to be one of our most valuable tools." The letters that parents write during the weekend often become "love letters to their kids." Also, seeing the most hard-boiled parent experience tears as he or she writes is not uncommon. The closing ceremony is based on this part of the experience. In the follow-up meeting with each family a month later, Falzone and Neville place the issues contained in these messages on center stage as a way of beginning the dialogue.

Watching these two young women talk about their work and careers and watching them work the weekend retreat is an energizing experience. They had comparatively less educational preparation for such a complicated intervention and relatively fewer work or life experiences to draw upon as they undertook the complex task of figuring out how to change a dysfunctional family across the course of a 24-hour weekend period. But while they might have been short on credentials and age, they were part of a person-centered system that encouraged excellence through creativity and personal development. Like others here, they were expected to change themselves for the better as they designed opportunities for clients to also change in positive ways. But, has their experience with the Oasis model been exclusively positive? Has theirs been an ideal success story? The answer is "of course not." As is the case with all parts of the center and the people who work there, Falzone and Neville endured some discomforts and were at times thrown off track by some of the agency's weaknesses. The loss of their third initial team member, Young, created a hole in their weekend synergy. The initial three could almost anticipate one another's reactions to families who were participating in the weekend experience. Other Oasis counselors willingly filled in for Young's absence, but Falzone and Neville recognized the loss of seamlessness that they experienced.

A Philosophy for Nonprofit Employee Growth   Judy Freudenthal has been at Oasis since its beginning as the agency that the community knows today. She is on the Management Team and functions as the director of counseling. Freudenthal is one of those people whose original vision gave importance to the idea that those who serve and encourage growth need to be served and encouraged to grow themselves. Freudenthal struggles with this philosophy and its consequences almost as much today as she did a dozen years ago. Like so many others at the agency, she is not one to rest on her laurels. Self-reflection and continual improvement are an important part of the culture. Freudenthal is considered by some to be the master instigator of the Oasis approach to ferreting out organizational weaknesses and potential land mines before they become too big to easily disable. "Prevention is about taking care of yourself and taking care of the organization," she says. "We can't expect people who are burdened by their employer to give adequate guidance and support to those who are trying to unburden themselves."

Emphasis on self-development at Oasis arises from the agency's belief that it is extremely difficult to teach what you do not know how to practice. Personnel see themselves as being in the business of encouraging people to grow as individuals and creating better environments for themselves. How odd, they reason, to expect that you could teach a beleaguered wife how to fashion a better family environment for herself if you cannot create a better organization within which to operate yourself. How inappropriate it would be to challenge a client to grow as a person through family and work if you were not learning how to respond to your own growth challenges through family and work. "Everybody gets stuck," Freudenthal says. All kinds of people get stuck in bad habits, bad relationships, and hurtful jobs and careers. "When we make the mistake of thinking we're different than our clients—that our humanness is different from theirs—we cannot empathize and we cannot effectively counsel," Freudenthal says. She articulates the agency's philosophy by referring to some of the expectations. "We need to be as responsive to our own growth needs as we are to the those of the clients," she says. "If we work on our relationships, we become better teachers of that sort of thing and we model for our clients better ways of communicating and problem-solving. We believe that's what a nonprofit organization ought to do." Out of this philosophy grows a commitment to the individual employee that rivals the organization's commitment to its clients. In subsequent chapters, we describe how the board and community have dealt with this novel approach. As the reader can well imagine, the birth and nurturing of this point of view has not been without its moments of discomfort and difficulty.

Family Support   Having been on board for only three years, Jill Baker is one of the newest associates at Oasis. As the director of Independent Living, Baker has direct management responsibilities for one of the teams. She told us that since coming to Oasis, she has learned to like her work in a way that had never before been possible. Baker explains that in former positions, she had often felt torn between her work and family responsibilities. At Oasis, her dual roles ceased to be a problem. "I don't worry anymore about my kid getting sick. This agency understands that parents have responsibilities for sick kids and so we encourage one another to do the right thing," she says. Often, Baker—like others—brings her ill child to work, but when that is not possible, she does not hesitate to stay home if that is the right solution to the temporary crisis. "This kind of attitude—a guilt-free support of family loyalties—makes me like my work more," she says. "I'm more effective."

Ken Chiccotella, the accounting coordinator, says that "no staff member ever left Oasis because the agency wouldn't work to help reduce conflicts coming from multiple roles." An undisputed reality at the center is that people do not criticize one another for dealing with family responsibilities during regular work hours. Coworkers do not complain, and management does not offer negative consequences. Thus, people routinely bring kids and pets to work, take kids and pets to medical appointments, make personal daytime visits to legal and government agencies, and even get the tires on their cars rotated during agency hours when necessary. During the course of our investigation, we heard anecdotes related to family support that involved computer repair, automobile repair, haircuts, giving blood, school conferences, medical appointments, therapy appointments, out-of-town guests, school pageants, and the need to accompany a spouse to an out-of-state business meeting.

The mechanism that makes it possible for people to accomplish these family events during agency hours is rather simple. Like a well-known advertising campaign suggests, they "just do it." Employees make their own decisions about what needs to come first: work or family. If they decide in favor of a family responsibility, they also decide how work at Oasis will be covered in their absence. A staff member might reschedule a meeting or ask a colleague to cover for them. Associates might ask a client to meet in a more convenient and time-saving location. They might ask if it is acceptable to bring a child or a pet to a conference. They might take work home or come in on the weekends in order to make sure that the Oasis job is completed.

Of all of the personal and professional supports in place at Oasis, this family-support component is perhaps the least problematic. It simply is not a big deal. Yet, we might wonder whether the staff is tempted from time to time to take advantage of the agency and community—to take time away from work in order to indulge hobbies or pander to laziness. As researchers, we had to consider the possibility that the people at this agency supported one another in a practice that ultimately resulted in defrauding the board, community, and funding sources. We were gratified to discover that we could find no data to support such a hypothesis. Staff personnel at Oasis tend to be strongly committed to their work—most often, working longer hours than required and occasionally foregoing vacation days in order to deal with a client crisis or mounting paperwork. Programs continually develop and proliferate at the center. Clients and community representatives talk about each associate in ways that let us know that these people are present and important factors in their lives. In fact, across the multi-year duration of our study, no member of another agency or government body in the Nashville area ever mentioned that one of Oasis's weaknesses was that people shirked professional duty in favor of family roles or personal indulgence. On several occasions, however, we did talk to people outside the agency who were aware of the family-support element, thought it strengthened the associates' levels of commitment, and wished that they could function in their jobs in a similar way. At no point did we discover that this family-support factor pulled people away from the center's goals. Our informants believe that this approach contributes to the Oasis success story in a major way.

We are becoming more and more aware that a growing number of contemporary companies are moving toward "the family thing" (Arnold & Plas, 1993; & Autry, 1992). Commonly, we will find for-profit organizations that support the family responsibilities of their employees. Like Oasis, they reason that multiple roles are a fact of life and that highly competent people seek out responsibilities in a variety of venues, such as work, family, volunteer service, and athletics. Smart companies make the employee aware that the organization feels an obligation to help minimize conflicts between home and work. So, as the century closes, the Oasis commitment to family is not particularly unique. What is unique, perhaps, is the additional step that this agency takes. Staff members at the center do not merely support one another's decisions in these matters—rather, they also encourage each other. One staff member told us about a particularly hectic month in which her attention to her own needs as well as to her family's needs habitually took a back seat to agency work. Without thinking, one day in an after-school telephone call, she told her junior high school-age child that she realized it would be impossible to pick him up after basketball practice. She told him that unfortunately, for yet one more day, he would have to find a ride home with another family. This staff member was startled when a member of the Management Team who had overheard her asked her point-blank if she was sure that decision was the correct one. If she had to decide to let her son find his own rides for a few weeks, was she planning to make that up to him and to change her practices of working late next month? Had she really taken the time to think through the situation with the attention that it deserved? Our informant told us that this concept is what the essence of family support is all about. Endorsing the decisions that staff members make about home and work conflicts is fine, but you know that the organization is truly committed to the successful resolution of these difficulties when people do not merely rubber stamp your decisions. At Oasis, they are more proactive than that by routinely encouraging you to consider your family's needs. By the way, this particular staff member reports that she surprised her son with a personal pick-up that day—and after that, she made it a personal habit to try to do so on most occasions throughout his basketball-practice season.

Acceptance

Encouragement for growth requires an acceptance of an associate's choices and values, skill levels, personal style, and short- and long-term goals. Our investigation revealed that this part of the organization's person-centered philosophy was one of the most difficult to realize, yet one of the components that is currently most firmly in place. Oasis staff members explained to us that really, it is not possible to encourage people to develop and to learn new things if you are unwilling to accept them for who they are. The organization must be prepared to support an individual's decision not to change, although change seems warranted. If that kind of acceptance is not in place, any support for change can legitimately be viewed as a demand for change.

Growth must always be a personal choice. If growth is extrinsically mandated, people are not likely to respond positively. Support becomes coercion. Thus, it is understood at this growth-oriented agency that times exist in which people need to remain within the perceived safety of the familiar. Likewise, with many people there will always be personal issues that are never available for intervention. When Baker reflects on the comparison between her two most recent employers, she says, "Coming where I came from, this is, like, the greatest! To be respected where you're at, for who you are, amazes me and inspires me."

Oasis associates believe that respect matters. When you truly respect people, you offer support but allow them to move at their own pace. Acceptance conveys respect for an individual's decision about what is best for him or her. "There is a feeling of warmth and caring," says Frances Rich. "When I made changes in my presentation skills I never felt pushed to do something I wasn't ready for," she says. Frances says that Sherry Allen, the director of the shelter and her immediate supervisor, "lets you know what you need to change, but doesn't devalue you. She always suggests ways of jointly solving the problem. Then, if you're not quite ready, that's okay, too."

Acceptance also extends to religious and lifestyle preferences. People who think independently about politics, spirituality, and family structures are not uncomfortable at Oasis. Embracing individual differences comes rather easily to most staff members. Those who arrived with less-flexible attitudes quickly committed themselves to learning the kind of tolerance for individual differences that is now a widely known characteristic of this agency.

Bette Shulman, a Counseling Team member, told us that acceptance of one another is a value that bleeds over into their work with clients. She says the heart of their approach to teen-agers is formed by a belief that "who the kids *are* is more important than passing seventh grade or stealing a car. If the agency treats them with acceptance then they will learn to value others that way. That is what really matters. We try to run our agency the way we want our kids to run their lives—with caring, respect, acceptance, and a commitment to becoming, each day, a better person."

Productive Confrontation

The Oasis Center was not the first nonprofit position that Paige McClain, a member of the Educational Services Team, landed after obtaining her master's degree. When she talked with us, she frequently mentioned other work as she described her current levels of comfort and productivity. When asked her opinion of Oasis's biggest strength, she did not hesitate. "I used to work with rude, intimidating people," she says. "Here, I work with nice people. The difference is in the way we handle problems. Here, we can just go tell one another what we think and what's bothering us. You can go to someone and tell them you're mad. There, everybody hid everything and talked behind backs and treated you rudely, but never dealt with the issues." When we asked if she meant that it is not uncommon at Oasis to hear someone yelling at another, McClain replied, "No. I've never heard much of that at all. Surely someone yelled once in a bad moment, but that wouldn't be common." In this agency, a cultural norm that encourages staff to confront problem-solving and style issues seems to result in the absence of two extreme coping measures: loss of temper and passive aggression. The unwritten rules for addressing intra-agency dynamics seem to require information-seeking and/or mature confrontation.

Suzanne Rhinehardt describes the management style of her supervisor, Rebekah Walker, as "confrontational without being confrontational. She expects me to take responsibility for my work and actions, but she's nurturing and gently pushes."

Probably the most common interpersonal discomforts within any organization revolve around misunderstandings. People easily interpret and misinterpret actions, words, and the absence of actions and words. Freudenthal says that when problems occur, most people at Oasis have learned not to assume a level of judgment that might not be there; rather, they obtain more information. Staff members commonly ask questions such as the following:

- Did that exasperated look this morning mean that I've let you down on this?

- Is it fair to conclude that I'm not going to be needed on this project?

- When you said that I ought to get involved in a relationship in-service, did you mean that I was ready to get even better—or did you mean that I'm seriously retarded in this?

- Does your lack of attendance at these meetings mean that you're disinterested in this stuff or maybe bored?

- Have I been too pushy on this thing lately?

Peggy Christian reports directly to Betty Everett, the Educational Services coordinator. "Anytime I go to Betty, we work complaints through and we work them out," Christian says. "Betty's just great, and like most people here, that's because she listens." Falzone and Neville, the Weekend Retreat Team, echo this sentiment. They told us that when complaints are voiced, things happen. "This place *does* respond to feedback," they say. Some of the methods of response are fairly innovative. For example, a Shelter worker, George Mensah, talked quite a bit about the retreats that the shelter staff has from time to time. They share such things as paddle boating, small training sessions, good food, and honest conversation. Mensah told us that communication problems are often addressed during these weekends, and people share information that makes it much easier for others to understand what they are thinking.

Productive confrontation involves more than just routine complaints and information seeking. When misunderstandings or frustrations tend to get in the way, uncomfortable staff members are expected to confront the issue in a mature way that involves scheduling appropriate talk time, issuing a clear statement of the problem, making a commitment to find a mutually agreeable solution, and not engaging in name calling. In other words, you are not likely to hear someone say:

- We have to talk about this right now!

- You've just been acting too weird!

- You'd better change!

- You jerk!

Rather, we commonly hear someone asking for time to talk; indicating that a specific behavior or attitude was troublesome; asking how responsibility for the problem might be partially hers or his; and dealing with the incident within a context of mutual respect.

Sherry Allen's take on this issue reveals another important fact about the Oasis approach to confrontation: often, a team is involved. In other words, a team is the object of the confrontation. Or, an individual who has been directly questioned often will respond to the issue not as an individual who is under fire, but from a team member's point of view. As a result of experience with this kind of direct problem-solving of intra-agency misunderstandings and conflicts, Allen believes the "teams are now more thick-skinned. Now, we're likely to assume a problem is a system problem rather than a personal attack."

Sherry also says that people have learned to reduce the impact of temporary style discomforts. People are much less likely to be disturbed about small things or to confront others about them. For example, she says that someone might comment, "Oh, no big deal. She's just PMSing about what to wear to the Artists for Oasis show." This much-respected supervisor told us that just that week, she had heard a colleague arrive at work in the main building with the announcement, "I'm having a terrible morning and I'm going to be bitchy. Let me know if I get out of hand." In some ways, that announcement captures the essence of this cultural norm and its effect on the agency. Individuals such as the speaker are expected to monitor their own senses of well-being. While an individual is not pressured to change an emotional experience or to pretend happiness and contentment when clearly those conditions are not present, they are expected to take responsibility for the effects of that experience on others. Announcing where they are coming from emotionally is standard operating procedure for people throughout Oasis. Asking others to give feedback if they are negatively affected by a mood difficulty is, quite commonly, part of the coping method of choice. The speaker that morning knew that the staff could be counted on to do as she asked, to let her know whether her mood was interfering with agency and personal agendas for that day.

When people make mistakes, this part of the culture makes it easier to avert the emotional response. Allen talks about how staff members come to accept some of their weaknesses as "just a fact of life," not giving the little things undue importance. Because they know that colleagues will mention the bigger issues, people can avoid unnecessary guilt trips over the small stuff.

One of the clearest expressions of the philosophy underlying the value of productive confrontation came during discussions with counselor Rebekah Walker. "One of the things we've learned for ourselves and teach to others is that talking never hurts permanently," she says. "It's the secretiveness that hurts. Getting it out into the open gets it down to size and makes it available for intervention. Sometimes, this is a *walking through fire*. It's hard, but it is so very worthwhile."

Empowerment　The second foundational component of the Oasis model results in respect and development of each staff member's chosen areas of expertise. "Basically, I'm running my own area," McClain says. "I'm my own boss with a great supervisor to bounce things off." McClain knows that her supervisor, Betty Everett, is going to serve her rather than dictate to her. McClain understands that if success in her area of educational services is to emerge, she is the one who will have to create that success. Oasis administration is not going to stand in her way. In fact, the situation is quite the contrary. Empowerment at this agency consists of a shared cultural norm. In other words, individuals are encouraged and expected to make decisions for the agency and for themselves. Those decisions are typically not questioned, almost always supported, and frequently applauded.

Professional Empowerment   Sharon Carter at Juvenile Justice remarks that so many of the Oasis success stories are born because "people over there take ownership. You don't expect mountains of red tape, but you do know that individuals are going to make decisions and create programs, if that's what it takes." While co-creating the Weekend Family Retreat program, Neville believes that she came to understand the dynamic that makes the difference. "Because the center values you and empowers you it reminds you to value and empower you," she says. Allen references a famous John F. Kennedy quote as she makes an important point about empowerment at Oasis: "We ask, why not?"

This agency abounds with personal success stories about skills learned and recognition won. Accounting Coordinator Ken Chiccotella points out that "in another organization, I'd only be doing accounting and the only skills I'd be improving would be accounting skills. Here, the empowerment emphasis results in my wearing many hats—and I like that." In addition to keeping the books, Chiccotella designs accounting systems for the center; participates in center strategy meetings; helps with carpentry and mechanical difficulties; and thinks about the center's weaknesses and suggests ways to improve things. In fact, finding a staff member who is not similar to Chiccotella is difficult. Almost all staff members who have been at the center for at least a year have reaped the results of the empowerment strategy that is fundamental to the Oasis person-centered leadership model.

Irma Ecksel works in the Transitional Living program, running interference in the community at large for older adolescents who are working to achieve independent citizen status with a job, housing, transportation, education, and a plan for the future. Ecksel finds the Oasis management style empowering. "I like working independently," she says. "It allows me to use my own initiative. No one ever says, 'Oh, but you can't.' What seems like little supervision is a way of care-taking—giving you room to grow." Ecksel adds, "I found my niche at Oasis. I am amazed how much I like it and how good I am at it."

Michelle, as we will call her, is a Caucasian middle-class girl who was thrown out of her house simply because she chose to date African-American men. Through the Independent Living program, she was able not only to complete high school, but to also earn a scholarship for college study.

Michelle eventually went on to graduate school. While achieving rigorous academic goals, she worked two jobs and bought a new car. At Oasis, Michelle found people who believed in her, supported and encouraged her, and highlighted her strengths. At Oasis, Michelle was empowered to succeed within the life of her choice.

Ecksel also recalls a recent visit from now 22-year-old, Casey. At 18, Casey was on suicide watch at the center. She painted her room black and destroyed the girls' bathroom at school with graffiti. With her negative, depressed outlook, Casey dragged others down with her. The Oasis Independent Living program gave Casey a safe place to turn her life around and to begin to see the positives in life. "Boy, if I knew then what I know now!" said Casey. "You ought to have me back there as a speaker!" Knowing Oasis, we expect that it will.

Rebekah Walker told us about a woman—let's call her Bonnie—with whom she had been working in a counseling capacity for a couple of years. The client's accomplishments included leaving a physically abusive relationship, learning how to communicate with her unhappy and violence-prone son, removing guns from her world, getting a decent paying job, and perhaps most importantly, turning to face and assimilate her past as an abused child. Walker asked Bonnie to co-lead a series of group counseling sessions with her. She believed that Bonnie had come so far that it would be a waste not to put opportunities for assisting others in her path. The center did not second-guess Walker's judgment in this matter, and the sessions turned out quite successfully. As Oasis empowers its staff members, they in turn empower their clients.

Personal Empowerment   The levels of empowerment at Oasis meet or exceed those of the most successful corporate organizations that have dedicated themselves to empowerment through a continuous-improvement management model. Not only do Oasis people make decisions about clients and programs, but they also make critical decisions about how they will function at the agency. Oasis people set their own hours. While staff members tend to work more than the expected 40 hours per week, they decide when those hours will be devoted to center work. Of course, exceptions to this norm exist—typically associated with the 24-hour, seven-day-a-week Shelter Program—where client needs demand that staff be available at specific times. Those personnel who do not have such specific commitments, however, allow themselves the flexibility to come and go as they please. Thus, a counselor might see clients on a Saturday afternoon, plan program adjustments with a colleague on the following Tuesday evening, and take all day Wednesday off. An Educational Services coordinator who begins the day at 10 A.M. during the summer in order to accommodate a family child-care schedule might work a few Saturday mornings in the fall. An individual whose 20-year Florida family reunion is coming up might work longer hours each day in order to get the decks clear enough to leave town for the three-day-long event. While accommodations for personal and professional needs such as these are not uncommon across the workforce today, the way in which Oasis deals with this sort of arrangement might well be quite atypical for a non-profit sector organization. Actually, the center does not deal with this sort of issue at all. The only time that anyone on the staff is made aware of such an accommodation is when someone is asked to cover for the individual. Also, this accommodation is revealed when team members are told about a new work schedule so that they can be forewarned or can elect to join after-hours or weekend planning sessions or programmatic events. These nonprofit workers have decided that this use of time is sensible. The flexibility means that the agency is family friendly and that clients who cannot participate from 8:30 A.M. to 4:30 P.M. during the week can be seen.

Empowerment and Burnout   Perhaps even more astonishing is the agency's formal and informal attitude toward potential burnout. These workers are not just encouraged to take care of themselves—they are *expected* to do so. They also expect one another to realize that they are in a high-burnout occupation because client needs are so basic, so huge, and so profound. Because they cope on a daily basis with violence, abuse, neglect, poverty, ignorance, racism, and seemingly impossible odds, these professionals constantly remind one another to be vigilant about their own emotional needs. Personal emotional overloads are eased in large part by the opportunities for growth and empowerment. Another important weapon in the constant battle against burnout is mental-health time. Staff members are expected to take time off when the pressures become too great, and they encourage one another to take this time off long before things become so bad that they boil over. Thus, it is not uncommon to learn that an individual has decided to take two weeks off for rehabilitation. Not infrequently, staff members might bail out of the work environment for an afternoon, a day, or a couple of days. The most important point to realize about this sort of mental-health break is that these occasions are expected and encouraged, rather than merely tolerated. People in the organization cannot recall an occasion when a staff member abused this privilege. These are dedicated professionals who love their work, their clients, and their employer. On any given day, they are more likely to work overtime than they are to work less time.

Oasis people sometimes adjust their schedules for reasons other than personal emotional overload and burnout, however. As the decade draws to a close, it seems that the staff has become just as serious about prevention as it is about rehabilitation. Freudenthal, the director of counseling services, plans for serious physical-fitness time somewhere within each week. Like others at Oasis and around the globe, she has learned that regular fitness activities keep her mentally and physically upbeat and less prone to colds and influenza attacks. Although it has been extremely difficult for her, she has learned to turn down a suggestion for an important problem-solving or planning meeting in favor of a previously scheduled physical-fitness hour at that particular time. When she originally devised this prevention plan, she most commonly gave up the fitness activity if an issue emerged that needed her attention. Eventually, she realized that there were always issues that needed her attention, and thus, her fitness goals were never met. So, little by little, she began to hang tough—to say, "No, I can't right now because I have to work out if I'm going to hold on to sanity this week." Freudenthal now feels the difference that this prevention strategy makes in her personal and professional selves. She becomes tired less frequently and has not felt the need for a week's rehabilitation in many months.

Empowerment at Oasis resides in the staff's ability to make personal and professional decisions that affect client welfare and their own performance. Perhaps the most important aspect of the Oasis empowerment philosophy, however, is just now being realized as more associates begin to focus on enabling themselves to *prevent* overload problems long before they occur. People such as Freudenthal are beginning to anticipate the negative consequences of long hours spent in response to society's most difficult and painful human problems, and they are taking pressure breaks that have proven effective in the quest for prevention of emotional overload and burnout.

Youth Empowerment   Let's not forget the hallmark of the Oasis model: staff associates practice the management philosophy that we are describing not only for personal and professional development, but primarily so that it can be imparted to the youth whom they serve. Clients are not merely provided services as passive recipients, but they are challenged to make a positive difference. Oasis received the 1997 Leadership in Building Youth Participation award from the National Network of Runaway and Youth Services. As previously mentioned, two youths are serving as full, voting board members. Additionally, Peer Educators volunteer to answer the crisis call line and participate in street-outreach activities. Peer-educator candidates are selected through a screening process that of course includes another peer educator. Ninety-five percent of these persons complete the 28-hour training program and volunteer on the crisis call line once or twice a week for three months. Peer educators also respond to media requests, having been trained by a board member who is skilled in public relations. This situation provides yet another opportunity for board members and youth to interact. The Peer Educator program is the brainchild of Cyndi Cass and represents one more example in which staff is empowered to create and use personal and professional resources at their disposal. Cass came to Oasis with a bachelor's degree and wanted to create a niche that her formal education level would not hinder. She had started a rape hotline while in college and had experience working with volunteers. "At Oasis," Cass states, "individual ideas are embraced. I wanted an innovative program structure where young people can blossom and feel listened to. Here, they are taken seriously."

The newest initiative, *Alternative Spring Break* (ASB), is organized in conjunction with the local YMCA. Students are involved in an intensive, week-long community-service experience, such as youth recreational programs on a Sioux reservation, hurricane cleanup, repair and rehabilitation of senior citizens' homes, and environmental protection work. Mike Cheatham, an Alternative Spring Break student, says, "I came to [my ASB project] with my problems and so did other people with me. It was a true experience for me. I've decided to go again next year. I just want to thank Jane, Scot, and the rest of the group for showing me a good time in learning and also in life."

Freudenthal, Oasis clinical director, notes that "research indicates there are four primary factors that contribute to young people staying out of trouble: 1) a sense of competence; 2) a sense of usefulness; 3) a sense of belonging; and 4) a sense of power. . . We must find ways to engage them as contributors within our community so that they have opportunities to develop positive self-perceptions and important skills in living." Oasis associates experience empowerment in their own lives, which translates to the lives of those they serve.

Team-Building

Various writers (Gardenswartz & Rowe, 1994; O'Brien, 1995; & Tjosvold & Tjosvold, 1991) have enumerated characteristics of successful teams. We are not redundant when we note that the traits of successful teams mirror other aspects of the Oasis model. What works well individually must also work well collectively. We found that the Oasis teams emulate what we conclude are the most important among these traits. In Chapter 8, "The Shelter: Against All Odds," we will discuss these factors and Oasis teams in more detail. As an overview, however, our critical elements for successful Oasis teams—or teams in general—include the following:

Goal Clarity and Commitment to Mission   Oasis literature repeatedly promotes the slogan that the agency "helps teens succeed." Individual program teams have a clear vision of how their specific program fosters that overarching goal and fits uniquely into the Oasis mission. Moreover, team understanding about missions and goals is not a "been there, done that" affair. Team meetings frequently revisit the important question of their specific tasks and how they can help teen-agers succeed.

Importance of Individual as Well as Team Growth   As conceptualized in Part One, teams in western society must not lose sight of individual development as well as success of the team project or goal. Oasis teams spend considerable energy nurturing the individual, making certain that all voices and ideas are heard, and supporting that process.

Flexibility: Willingness to Change   This principle is important at both the team and the individual levels. Adapting to the ever-changing needs of teen-age clients requires an openness to try new approaches. Each client presents a unique set of circumstances, life skills, and family variables—and no cookie-cutter approach will reach everyone.

Trusting Relationships   Team trust is fostered through physical proximity, personal sharing, team time spent away from the job, and laughter. Praise and encouragement is generous and sincere.

Willingness to Confront   This characteristic balances the nurturing, positive praise which is also critical. Because of its caring environment, Oasis teams struggle with confrontation but are generally able to do so in non-threatening ways.

Acceptance of the Team   Management must not second-guess the team's decisions. Team autonomy, balanced with accountability, will foster empowerment and a sense of self-directedness for program teams.

THE BEGINNING: HOW DOES THE LEADERSHIP
START A PERSON-CENTERED PROCESS?

What we described previously is the model that we initially encountered, refined as a result of the growth that the agency experienced throughout the 1990s. This model does not tell the whole story, however. When we sent a draft of this book to field and academic practitioners for comment and review, an observation that we received from two individuals seemed particularly cogent. They wrote something to this effect: "But, how did the leadership begin this process? How did this model emerge within this particular setting?"

We had not included information about this important issue originally, because our research project had not been designed to elicit historical data. We took the position that we were interested in the Oasis management model, how embedded the model is within the organization, and how it affects agency outcomes—without reference to how it was originally engendered. We now realize that we were remiss in neglecting this important historical piece of information, particularly because it could be of some use to other nonprofit organizations embarking on the development of their empowerment models. Therefore, we revisited our information banks for this project in order to provide at least some perspective on the important topic of the Oasis model's birth process. Re-inspection of the data revealed the presence of many observations about the history of the organization from people within the agency, as well as former board members and community leaders. Although the observations discussed in the following sections did not arise from research questions that were designed to elicit historical data, we nonetheless believe that these impressions are sound and worthy of mention because of the material about the beginnings of the model that we found within our data sets.

In Retrospect

During the mid and late 1980s, Oasis staffers at all levels involved themselves with local and regional training, as did many nonprofit personnel all over the country. Professional development has always been important for social service workers, and this agency proved no exception in that regard. Originally within this field, in-service workshops (so-called trainings) typically focussed on clinical skills and client-service agendas. With the advent of participatory management came a trend toward diversification of these in-service events in that during that period, all over the country, some of them began to focus on management strategies. People at Oasis attended their fair share of this training. During the early '90s, chief among those approaches that particularly appealed to those who were in Oasis executive and leadership positions was a series of experiences on the Learning Organization (Chawla & Renesch, 1995; & Senge, 1990 & 1994) and a variety of workshops on team-based management and service (for example, Heller, 1998; & Holpp, L., 1999). The leadership in place at that time decided that a team-based reorganization of the center might meet the agency's needs. They put this suggestion in front of individuals all over the agency. A series of staff meetings resulted in the establishment of a team-based approach. Then, the fun began.

The agency began to experience the same sort of discomforts that so many other organizations encounter as they move to a team approach (refer to Part One and Chapter 9, "A Vital and Vibrant Infrastructure: Teamwork that Works"). Many of the individuals who were in Oasis leadership positions at that time were rather persistent people who committed themselves and the agency to a genuine solution for the problems of team-based functioning. Meeting after meeting ensued; teams met; the staff met; and programs took place. They tinkered. The team strategies that they had read about and learned in various workshops were redesigned to fit their own setting and goals.

Chief among the early strategies that seemed clearly important to these individuals was a demand for open communication. They agreed that hidden agendas did not serve good purposes. They challenged one another to open debate, to a public airing of grievances that might be getting in the way. They also challenged one another to ride through this stage. They even hoped in those early days that an occasionally stormy session might merely constitute a stage that they would eventually overcome. They have since learned that occasional storms are far preferable to unexpressed hostilities and back-biting and that they are a rather predictable part of growth and change within communities. As we reported previously, now they have institutionalized openness within their public forums in such a way that airing grievances becomes a rather routine part of baking the daily bread.

The Leaders

The role that many in the identified leadership positions of that time set for themselves was one of information provider, enabler, and facilitator.

People all over the agency were encouraged to attend relevant training. Those who did were expected to share within in-service events at the agency.

As individuals, these leaders encountered predictable role confusion and feelings of anxiety. Chief among these was concern over just what it meant to give the power away, to entrust everyone at the agency with goal setting, programmatic design, and strategic planning. For all participatory leaders, facing up to these concerns can constitute a very critical stage in the process. Empowerment becomes especially worrisome in the early stages as an organizational leader faces the expectations of his or her governing board or some other higher-up within the system. Oasis leaders were no exception in this regard. Their concerns centered on their responsibilities to the board of directors. Would the sort of empowerment that was occurring seem irresponsible to the board? In part, the leadership dealt with this issue in those days by not dealing with it. At points throughout the development of the model, the board was simply not completely aware of the participatory nature of all of the staff's programmatic and structural arrangements. While there was no direct attempt to withhold information from the board, the organization's staff and leadership had not been in the habit of challenging traditional board-agency expectations and functioning. As we mention in Chapter 6, "Strengths and Weaknesses: Growing Pains and Growing Satisfactions," and describe in detail in Chapter 7, "The Board of Directors: The Creation of a New Participatory Model," the fact that the organization did not challenge these traditional expectations became a critical problem. The organization was limited at one point in its capability to grow because an important part of the entity, its board of directors, had not been empowered within the participatory model that had taken such firm hold on the organization. As you will discover in Chapter 7, eventually this developmental difficulty was remedied.

The Turn Toward the Individual

Articulation of the person-centered model that is now the reality grew from the early discussions of how team-based functioning might actually be made effective within this agency. Every time they changed a dynamic or structure, it seemed that they ran into a professional-personal issue of some sort that belonged to an individual. The teams reasoned that they could not proceed successfully if they did not support the individual's current growth needs. So, they stopped what they were doing for the team, the organization, and the client, and turned their attention and resources toward the team member. This sort of thing was occurring all over the agency within all teams.

What happened at that point was rather simple and can be summarized with a single word: success. The more the agency paid attention to the individuals who worked within it, the better the teams worked and the better the programming became. Grants and recognition began to trickle their way. They began to get more community referrals. They began to be cited as a model of achievement around town. Most important, teen clients and their families began to succeed.

At about this time, some three or four years into the team project, the organization made that latter achievement the agency's motto: "Where teens succeed." Also around that time, the organization realized that when it stopped to pay attention to the needs of the individual associate, it was not really stopping at all. An awareness began to dawn that paying attention to individual employee needs was part of the empowerment process and perhaps the most crucial part of their management philosophy. The formal leader's new role became staying the course and opening communication lines.

The Formal Leader's New Role: Staying the Course, Opening Communication Lines   As you review this birth story, you can sense, we suspect, that unlike some other organizations, this organization did not intentionally set out to develop a new management strategy—and it certainly did not set out to develop a person-centered management model. The organization's original intent had been to try the new team approach to service. After encountering the problems that so many run into when moving toward a team-based model, the organization began to tinker with the strategies. Openness and persistence resulted in the development of a person-centered approach that required the organization to target associate growth needs at the same time that it targeted client needs. The formal leadership's role in the beginning was to facilitate, encourage, and perhaps most importantly, commit the organization to staying the course. Now, formal leadership roles are embedded within the team structure. As you will learn in Chapter 9, typical, traditional leadership responsibility and functions reside within the team. Even the executive director, who still retains certain unique fiduciary responsibilities vis-à-vis the board, is a member of the Management Team. As such, he shares responsibility with others on that team for serving the needs of the organization. As you will learn, the executive director of this organization is no longer the sole link between the board and the staff, and many of the communication and planning responsibilities traditionally located within the executive director position are now shared by teams all over the agency.

IN CONCLUSION

We found that one of the most obvious realities of the Oasis participatory model is that it is developed within and guided by the prevailing organizational culture. The philosophy and strategies are not handed down by senior management, nor are they typically developed by a committee of those who represent associates in various programs and at various levels. *All* associates participate in leadership and management decisions, particularly those that affect their areas of expertise and responsibility. Each does so at the same time that he or she strategizes regarding a personal and professional growth agenda and that of colleagues. This philosophy and method results in a culture that is deeply embedded within the extant management model. The culture does not operate in opposition to the prevailing culture nor parallel to it, as is the case in many non-participatory organizations as well as some participatory organizations that tend to emphasize teamwork over the individual.

In the following chapter, we talk about the strengths and weaknesses of the Oasis model and give you an overview of how the philosophies and strategies tended to operate across a multi-year period.

REFERENCES

Arnold, W. W., & Plas, J. M. (1993). *The human touch: Today's most unusual program for productivity and profit.* New York: John Wiley & Sons.

Autry, J. A. (1992). *Love and profit: The art of caring leadership.* New York: Avon.

Chawla, S., & Renesch, J. (Eds.). (1995). *Learning organizations: Developing cultures for tomorrow's workplace.* Portland, OR: Productivity Press.

Drucker, P. F. (1954). *The practice of management.* New York: Harper & Row.

Gardenswartz, L. and Rowe, A. (1994). *Diverse teams at work: Capitalizing on the power of diversity.* Chicago: Orwin.

Hoxie, E. D. (1918). *Scientific management and labor.* New York: Holt.

O'Brien, M. (1995). *Who's got the ball? A player's guide for work teams.* San Francisco: Jossey-Bass.

Senge, P. M. (1990). *The fifth discipline: The art and practice of the learning organization.* New York: Doubleday.

Senge, P. M. (1994). *The fifth dicipline fieldbook: Strategies and tools for building a learning organization.* New York: Currency.

Tjosvold, D. and Tjosvold, M. M. (1991). *Leading the team organization: How to create an enduring competitive advantage.* New York: Lexington Books.

6

Strengths and Weaknesses
Growing Pains and
Growing Satisfactions

A mere overview of the Oasis Center model, how it functions, and user attitudes toward the model—as found in the previous chapter—does not convey all of the most important information. Here and in following chapters, we present a description of its consequences—those positives and negatives that center associates, clients, and community partners experience on a daily basis as a result of this approach to person-centered leadership and management.

A COMMENT ON THE LONGITUDINAL NATURE
OF THE CASE STUDY

One century has become the next. The Oasis of the 20th century has become, in this century, a different entity. Change was a constant reality and continual expectation. Possibly, it is always true that much wisdom exists in the expectation that things will not remain the same for long within an organization—especially in one that is committed to struggle, growth, and vitality. Here, in addition to reporting our original findings, we share the results of the changes that occurred over time.

Longitudinal Methodology and Issues

As we discuss Oasis Center weaknesses and strengths, we talk about them as they developed across a five-year period in the life of the organization. We undertook three formal data-collection phases within this five-year longitudinal study. Between our formal phases of inquiry into Oasis and its culture, we casually followed the agency's progress through newsletters and occasional conversations with various associates.

The second data-gathering period occurred some 18 months after phase one, while the third occurred about a year after that. This longitudinal approach helped us understand how Oasis seems to be ever evolving and changing in response to internal and external needs, stresses, and opportunities.

During the second and third phases, follow-up questions (some practical, others theoretical) were designed to elicit information about the components of the Oasis model, including philosophy, strategies, and outcomes that we had learned about in the first data-collection phase. These questions were generated after deliberation about a series of issues that we thought were to consider after that initial phase:

- We had read about new programs, staff changes, and growth. Did the specialness of Oasis transcend these changes, or was it lost in the transition?

- Did this organization remain fundamentally person-centered, or did hierarchical management gain precedence?

- Did the Oasis culture consistently give large amounts of attention to staff development and welfare, or did this agency revert to an exclusive focus on the client population and the politics of funding, as tends to be the case in many traditional nonprofit organizations?

- What became of the challenges that were in the forefront at the outset of the study—issues that we raise as follows, such as low salaries, the need to relate differently with the board, and the lack of connectedness across program teams?

In short, we realized the need to go back to Oasis for a follow-up that would assess the robustness of the characteristics that we originally uncovered. Each time we returned, we assumed that the organization had changed, and we wanted to see how. We conducted our follow-up research with additional qualitative interviews as well as a small, secondary, quantitative measure of sense of community at Oasis.

Embedded within the following discussions of Oasis strengths and weaknesses, you will find observations on how the person-centered Oasis model that we described in the previous chapter has stood the test of time. We address the issue of the robustness of the model more directly at the close of this chapter.

An Approach to Organizational Positives and Negatives

Wherever a person-centered model is located—in a profit-making or nonprofit organization—you will find an emphasis on making personal and organizational weaknesses known. Strengths are equally important, and in some settings, it is more difficult for associates to talk about these strengths. Nonetheless, an emphasis on making the weaknesses available for comment and intervention is an important strategy in these sorts of organizations.

Traditionally, management wisdom led people to believe that it was smart to keep your weaknesses to yourself—as a person and as an organization. People assumed that the individuals who get ahead are the ones who play things close to their chests, holding information about defects and vulnerabilities just as tightly as information about the budget. With the advent of participatory management of all types, however, has come a letting loose of heretofore privately held data.

In person-centered organizations, we reason that a completely fundamental emphasis on revealing the vulnerabilities is crucial if success is to be achieved. Simply put, if you cannot obtain knowledge of your colleagues' weaknesses and your organization's defects, you cannot fix them or compensate for them. Therefore, at an agency such as Oasis, people do not often hesitate to admit their difficulties and to make them available for possible intervention. As researchers, throughout our investigation we were as interested in the handicaps as we were the capacities. Our method called for structured interview questions designed to reveal personal as well as system negatives and positives.

OASIS WEAKNESSES

The inadequacies we discovered during our longitudinal study of this organization fell into two categories: a concern common to most participatory models and those weaknesses unique to this center.

A Common Participatory-Management Concern

Oasis staffers complain about a problem that is shared by most other participatory-management organizations: taking an uncomfortably long time to make a group decision. While individuals and teams are empowered to think and act in a timely fashion, when the entire organization or significant parts of it needs to deliberate and decide, processes might grind along slowly. This problem is present in most participatory organizations, because involving people in decision making can take longer than when a decision is simply made at the top and is passed down. Sherry Allen, the former shelter director, puts it this way: "We're concerned about consensus and getting people on board. Therefore, we meet to death and we lose time. This pressures us to get the daily bread baked—especially here at the shelter, where 24-hour-a-day demands interfere with the amount of processing time we have available."

So, empowering individuals to make decisions has not resulted in an expected outcome, nor has it decreased the amount of time necessary to conduct the organization's business. True, this agency—like person-centered, profit-making corporations—has definitely decreased the amount of red tape and the number of forms and bureaucratic hoops that have to be negotiated. The truth is, however, that the time that people might have invested into officious endeavors has not been saved; rather, it is now offset by the increased time invested in activities such as consensus building, participatory decision-making, and focus sessions. In fact, it might be true that Oasis is spending more time on participatory management than it would have spent on bureaucratic management. As Allen points out, however, "Participation is necessary for agency and personal growth." In this organization—similar to others that have transitioned to this leadership style—associates far prefer putting time into partnership activities over going through motions that require red tape. While no net gain of time exists at Oasis, there is a gain in ownership, empowerment, creativity, and job satisfaction. A critical gain exists in strength of sense of community at the center. Nonetheless, time spent processing problems and decisions annoys Oasis associates from time to time. Those who are especially concerned about this problem appear to be younger employees who have never experienced a bureaucratic nonprofit organization and thus, are not in a position to compare weaknesses. Older, highly experienced administrators also tend to become frustrated a little more easily with this particular problem, because they know how to make good decisions and will occasionally long for the days when they could make them on behalf of the organization without consulting others. Yet, the critical point is that in this organization (as well as in other person-centered corporate environments), even those who become a bit wearied by the time necessary to build participation do not desire a return to bureaucratic, hierarchical management. Nonetheless, this agency believes that it needs to trail-blaze methods of streamlining communication so that participatory management will function more efficiently, but not be compromised.

Unique Oasis Concerns

A description of a person-centered organization is not fully accurate until the vulnerabilities of the system—which are so familiar to its associates—are made clear. While the weaknesses we are about to describe are particular to this organization at a specific stage in its development, we present these weaknesses with trust that the reader can generalize some of the lessons learned to other organizations at other stages of development. The fact that we pay attention to system defects in this report—and to associates during daily Oasis functioning—should not be construed to mean that this organization suffers from significant deficiencies that hamper its capability to perform. This situation is simply not the case. What is true is that this system, like all others, is affected on a daily basis by its positives and negatives. As one staff member, George Mensah, put it, "The work here is of such value that even the weaknesses that are most annoying can seem petty." While his positive attitude is shared by most at the center, it is also true that staff members take their deficiencies to heart, believing that an organization should commit itself to continual improvement in all areas—the weak *and* strong areas. The most significant weaknesses at the center have been associated with the ways in which the organization can become boxed in by its culture, funding woes, a communication breakdown among the organization's parts, attitudes toward strengths and weaknesses, and relations with the board.

Culture Traps

As we reported previously, this organization is committed to accepting diversity, encouraging personal growth, supporting risk-taking, and making personal positives and negatives available for comment and assistance. These people confront one another when they feel uncomfortable about a process or decision and encourage one another to think outside the box, working toward times when they can launch new programs that are capable of meeting entrenched and powerful societal problems. One of the consequences of this particular work ethic is somewhat disturbing to all of the people who participate in this work ethic. This accepting culture has not been able to welcome those who are not as open and accepting as those who are already on board. One associate made a decision that "was not the same as the ideals espoused." The more serious error, however, was the fact that this person "blew off a feedback session," despite this person's awareness that feedback is a cornerstone of Oasis culture. That associate is no longer with the organization. As the reader might imagine, this sort of situation often results in great discomfort for the agency, as well as for associates and new hires who do not quite fit in. You would not be so happy working at this agency if you were not willing to accept constructive criticism and to grow, risk, and create while accepting a multiplicity of lifestyle decisions. Eric Rhinehardt, an Oasis counselor, said it well: "We're embedded in our own culture." In other words, this extremely tolerant culture is intolerant of rigidity and the intolerant.

This culture cannot assimilate those who have fundamentalist persuasions; rather, it tends to provoke stress in those who are unmotivated to take risks. Yet, the center occasionally hires those people who have these traits. Typically, they eventually leave.

Some rather important catch-22 consequences result from the paradoxes that are inherent in this particular portion of the culture. This area has been one of the most consistently troublesome areas for the organization.

While the existence of this situation is a problem, equally difficult has been the center's response to this concern. Oasis associates beat themselves up about this issue on a regular basis. They are self-reflective enough that they recognized this culture trap—the intolerance of the tolerant toward intolerance—several years ago. So, they regularly catch themselves not practicing what they preach. They worry and wonder what this situation means. The agency is aware that it has a history of not having solved this problem, and it continually worries about (and suffers from) this conundrum at some level most of the time. We might say that the issue resides just beneath the surface, almost in the collective unconscious of the organization, influencing its sense of well-being as people admit that they who espouse acceptance cannot accept a certain kind of diversity.

At the end of the primary phase of our investigation of the Oasis organization, in feedback sessions with the staff, Management Team, and board, we offered a perspective on this problem. From our position as observers, it seemed to us that this particular problem was the result of organizational growing pains.

By definition, an organizational culture of any sort functions to exclude those who cannot participate effectively in that culture (Deal & Kennedy, 1982). An agency that wants to develop in profitable ways must monitor its culture carefully. Wisdom requires the organization to actively take steps to change the culture when a particular set of informal attitudes keeps the group from reaching its goals. The Oasis Center is clearly an organization that performs this sort of careful monitoring. So, given the agency's commitment to catching itself in the act of thwarting its own growth, and given its allegiance to its carefully crafted cultural norms, it seemed important for the organization to accept the reality that not all personalities and styles can function effectively in that sort of environment. The organization seemed best advised to accept the probability that a carefully crafted culture will, out of necessity, exclude those who cannot participate effectively. At the close of phase one of the study, many associates believed that as the organization matures, it might be in a position to accept more gracefully the limitations and potentials created by the management philosophy that it embraces.

Culture Trap: Follow-Up

At the close of the study, we revisited the issue. As of this writing, it seems that the center is still at the mercy of this set of dynamics.

THE ISSUE RESTATED   The organizational culture requires staff members to accept and encourage diversity among clients and staff. Thus, individuals and teams believe that all sorts of people should be given the opportunity to join the staff if their qualifications merit. Those who hold views in opposition to the prevailing Oasis culture would bring a breath of fresh air to the organization, giving it the vitality that occurs when differences come together in a common cause. Yet, what actually happens appears far from ideal. Occasionally, people have been hired who simply cannot endorse some of the basic Oasis norms. The religious beliefs of these staffers might make it impossible to deeply respect religious and lifestyle differences. They might not be able to endorse norms that push for personal growth and honest confrontation. Many at the center have found themselves confounded by the problem. How do you invite new blood into the center—people who have opposing views that might profitably change the prevailing culture—while maintaining a firm grasp on aspects of the culture that those already on board simply do not want changed? Early on, we received the impression that many of the mistakes that the agency reported to us centered on the problem of having hired people who simply could not endorse some of the critical, prevailing norms. Problems and strife ensued. While some staff members who were a good fit with the organization left for a variety of other reasons, others left because they could not—or chose not— to fit in.

CURRENT STATUS   This issue remains a confining conundrum. Associates are able to articulate the problem: Commitment to diversity and equality of opinion should not result in loss of the cultural norms that have made the organization so unique and so valuable to the community. On several occasions throughout the process of gathering information during the last phase of investigation, we heard people say that they simply needed to bite the bullet and lay claim to a right to endorse the cultural norms that have made the organization thrive. These staffers have said that Oasis norms that expect honest confrontation and dialogue, personal stretching, and commitment to diversity of lifestyle should be fully sanctioned once and for all, and that potential hires should be evaluated against this package of cultural standards (as well as against more conventional credentialing standards). Yet, as of this writing, it is quite unclear to us which path the organization will pursue. In this particular area, the organization seems to continue to lack vision and voice. Will Oasis continue to hire people who cannot endorse the values of the organization, resolving differences only as an individual sees fit? Those who prefer not to continue along this path point out that this resolution of the issue routinely results in failure on both sides—the individual and the agency. Or, is it likely that the agency will acknowledge a core set of values and hire those employees who are most likely to work well within its organizational culture? Interestingly, those who prefer not to take this second path might well be those who most passionately endorse the values, especially the basic value of acceptance. Or, will there be a third option? We will stay tuned.

Funding Woe: Low Salaries

At the time of this study, the most uncomfortable weakness that the agency faced was the inability to acquire adequate funding for its programs. The center's programs and impact on the community have grown geometrically over the past 10 to 15 years. Awards were won, grants were acquired, and significant funding was obtained through United Way and private foundations. Still, the center's programmatic efforts had not kept pace with the local demand for services, although new and old services were expanded. As the agency has stretched itself, program funding for current projects has been typically tenuous from year to year—even as community organizations ask for more service. Throughout our staff interviews, we heard associates reflect on how much they appreciated employment at this agency at the same time they were keenly aware of just how much they gave up in salary and security in order to be part of the operation.

Salaries at this agency have not been particularly competitive with salaries at other nonprofit organizations in the community. The funding base of most programmatic efforts has been unstable, often resulting in serious individual concerns about job security. Staff attrition rates ranged from 19 percent to 28 percent during 1997, 1998, and 1999. Employee exit questionnaires indicated that 31 percent of employees left for better pay. Of the staff members who completed the question, "How do you view your salary?" 62 percent felt that the salaries were below market value; 31 percent viewed them as average; and only 7 percent described them as competitive.

Notwithstanding these financial pressures, most associates echo the words of one relatively new member of the Oasis team: "I am generously nurtured here. So, it wasn't worth the extra money to go somewhere else when I got another job offer at an agency that not only isn't Oasis, it's not even basically team-based." Existing side by side with this sort of positive reasoning, however, has been an undercurrent of serious discontent about the financial insecurities of the agency.

Ken Chiccotella, the accounting coordinator, has noted that while a few people have left the agency because of problems fitting in with the organizational culture, most staff members who left had to go because their financial responsibilities required them to look for positions elsewhere that would pay the kind of salary that they could command. Sharon Carter at Juvenile Justice (and others) have worried that the agency might have tended to defeat its own diversity goals—because to some extent, Oasis has attracted people who had other sources of income and did not need to rely exclusively on their Oasis salary. We discovered that while the majority of staffers, regardless of their personal financial positions, have stayed with the agency, most came to feel the way Peggy Christian did a few years back when the announcement was made that there would be no raises for staff the following year. She felt that the situation was clearly unfair and unacceptable at the same time that she felt validated by her immediate supervisor, who shared her frustrations and bitterness. "Betty truly cared," Christian said. "The agency couldn't give us what we deserve. But management people like Betty took it as hard as we did."

All over the country, inadequate funding is typically a huge problem for social-service agencies. Yet, we were somewhat surprised to discover that this award-winning agency had not been able to use its creative juices to solve the funding woes that are so often associated with nonprofit organizations. We wondered, "If the agency can use its collective wit and wisdom to figure out ways to positively impact significant and entrenched social problems, such as delinquency, drug dependency, abuse, and family dysfunction, why has it not used these same strengths to solve problems of insecure funding patterns and inadequate salaries?" Eventually, we started asking this question of all Oasis personnel whom we interviewed. The answers we received pretty much fell into three categories: scarcity models, lack of experience, and old-fashioned bashfulness.

Scarcity Models   "Most agencies hold a scarcity model that always makes it hard to keep faith with social justice," says Bette Shulman. Others agree that Oasis personnel have fallen into the trap of believing that social concerns must inevitably take a back seat to other community priorities, such as corporate growth, profit motives, libraries, the arts, and attractive, quality housing. Shulman says that from time to time, many associates have lost faith in the basic validity and value of the Oasis mission as they thought about other community concerns and needs, such as safe streets, new interstates, and the desire of their neighbors to bring to town the *National Football League* (NFL), *National Hockey League* (NHL), and other sports franchises. The agency did not question seriously conventional community priorities. So, in many cases, Oasis did not move ahead with its dreams. The shelter building is a good case in point. Until a fire gutted the old building, people talked about a capital campaign to build a prototype center for homeless youth, but such a campaign just did not move from dream toward reality until disaster forced the issue. Allen, one of the center's most creative thinkers, nonetheless reflects a conventional scarcity model way of thinking as she says, "Oasis feels as stable as any nonprofit can, as far as money is concerned."

Whenever financial crisis looms—and that is often—Oasis people streamline, says Shulman. "We're good at that, but we haven't been good at being true to our dreams." In fact, in addition to being sharp when it comes to cutting corners and making do, Oasis has been quite good at certain kinds of fundraising. Jill Baker points out that she did not become anxious when she found out that half the funding for her position had been cut. She knew that she could rely on agency resourcefulness to solve the problem. Usually, Oasis figures out some way to cut a corner or piece together an approach that will keep a program going. Indeed, the agency has an enviable track record when it comes to getting government and private grants, as well as program award monies. In addition, Oasis has established an extremely successful community-based fundraising initiative called Artists for Oasis. Local artists donate works that are auctioned at an evening gala. In addition to capturing financial capital, the Artists for Oasis program gives the agency excellent community visibility. If the agency has been so good at gaining funding, however, why have funding woes been such a serious problem?

Rapid growth means that new and greater funding solutions also have to arrive rapidly. While associates were busy concentrating on staffing the newly expanded programs, they were not putting significant energy into figuring out how to support these programs. The unwitting acceptance of the scarcity model that Shulman talks about has played a large role in the problem. People at Oasis assumed that it *should* be difficult to get funding for social-service projects. They assumed that easy sources of revenue should be a consequence of quality profit-making enterprises, not the sort of work that is done at Oasis. While we heard people all over the agency talk about the need to transform the single part-time fund raising position into a full-time staff position, we only heard two Oasis associates talk about the need for the whole agency to get involved with brainstorming the financial problems. Presumably, an all-out effort on the part of all agency personnel would have to begin with a reassessment of the validity of holding a scarcity model, given the agency's objectives, talents, and dreams.

Inexperience   Most people at Oasis learned their professions and skills in academic programs that unconsciously adopted a scarcity model. They had not learned to question the fact that social-service organizations tend to be less well-funded than government or private organizations. As a result, they developed themselves for the most part within educational programs that did not provide coursework in nonprofit fiscal management. Furthermore, they were not encouraged (in or outside class) to think about possibilities for non-traditional agency funding. Therefore, these creative professionals had never before found themselves pressed to put their creative energies to work thinking about long-term funding possibilities for their agency.

Michael Heard, a board member, helped us think about this aspect of the problem. He believes that agency personnel had bought into a classic false dichotomy between the financial and service sides of the nonprofit organization. For example, creativity was reserved for service projects, and financial challenges were rarely greeted with the kind of enthusiasm routinely given to the challenges associated with child development and family dysfunction. Heard found that one of the biggest weaknesses at the agency was that associates were rarely driven by financial objectives. While the agency works within a consensus management mindset, historically the agency has not used consensus-management strategies when working on fiscal problems. Like many nonprofit workers all over the country, some Oasis associates were not trained (nor expected) to solve funding woes. At the time of our study, we could clearly see that this area of agency responsibility was the last to be submitted to the group's person-centered leadership tactics. At the time the core of our research project came to a close, people all over the center were just beginning to prepare themselves to make up for their lack of experience in long-term financial-management areas.

Bashfulness

Mary Huston McLendon was chairperson of the board at the time of our initial study. She spoke with enthusiasm about her respect and commitment for Oasis, and she also spoke frankly about her fiscal concerns. "These people hate to ask for money," she says. She talked of her amazement that such ingenious people—who will not hesitate to vigorously lobby anybody on behalf of a teen—should find themselves so at a loss when it comes to soliciting funds from the community's more advantaged citizens and corporations. She, as well as others, helped us to see that Oasis personnel were masters at asking for *things* but were really quite shy about asking for *dollars*. In other words, few had difficulty asking for donations of art, school supplies, food, clothing, and even time. They tended to have a great deal of difficulty asking for a monetary contribution, however. Again, this situation might relate to a scarcity mindset, to having overlooked the obvious fact that giving money to this stellar agency is, in many ways, a privilege. Here, your dollars have an opportunity to do real good.

In fact, we noticed a tendency on the part of Oasis personnel to downplay the specifics of their contributions to the community. In a lengthy interview with the board, we learned that associates rarely discussed cases or talked about success stories. At that time, board members tended to hear about the accomplishments of the agency from people in the community—families or agencies that had experienced great benefit from their association with the center. An in-depth look at this issue revealed that in part, this situation was a result of the strict code of ethics, especially confidentiality, at the agency. Staff members were reluctant to share stories of individual cases, even with names concealed, for fear that someone might deduce the true identity of the person being discussed. In addition to this ethical consideration, however, we discovered another dynamic at work: old-fashioned bashfulness. Many at Oasis just did not feel comfortable tooting their own horns. As they successfully adopted a humble approach to their accomplishments, however, they also made it difficult for the community to learn about the compelling reasons why this agency was well worth supporting financially.

As we finished examining the data that we gathered concerning this issue during phase one, it seemed clear that if this agency is to continue to grow and be responsible for the outstanding programs that it initiated, staff might well have to give up conventional attitudes toward nonprofit funding. As they relinquish a scarcity mindset and a bashful approach, while gaining greater experience in fiscal growth, they will need to use their creative energies to establish new ways of obtaining consistent and plentiful support for their work. Indeed, at the time our initial research phase was winding down, the agency had decided to pull everyone together to develop a strategic plan that would meet the center's funding needs for the long term.

Funding Woe: Follow-Up   When honest dialogue began, one of the first areas in which the board and staff went to work was staff salaries. At its most basic level, the problem was that these people worked for less than national or local norms. A capital campaign eventually gave a significant boost to front-line staff paychecks. Program development also received a firmer financial foundation. Even a year or so ago, people in all positions at Oasis commented on their satisfaction with salary levels. They were not being handsomely paid, but they were earning at least at an average rate. We thought that having taken the issue head on, the board and staff had worked together to resolve the inadequacies. Funding woes had ceased to be an agency weakness—at least, as indicated by the low 6 percent staff attrition in 2000 and compared to the double-digit figure the previous three years.

Now, however, one does not hear this sort of satisfaction when inquiring about salary levels. When we raised the issue in dyadic conversations or in group discussions at the beginning of this decade, a substantial amount of sighing could be heard. Grumbling appears to be possibly just beneath the surface. Inquiries of those who are most closely connected to financial matters have revealed that things seem to be cycling back to where they were five to 10 years ago. The problem seems to be that just a short time ago, another excellent equity plan was developed—but programmatic growth has been so great that in part, priority has recently been shifted to the need for additional staff positions, rather than existing salaries. Again, staff are feeling substantially appreciated in all ways except in this area—an area that is of fundamental importance for the quality of life for their families and for the pursuit of their personal dreams. As of this writing, we had not detected that any serious plan had yet been formed to deal (once again) with this important consideration. Oasis will be well served to keep its eye on salary and related attrition data now and in the future.

An Inter-Team Communication Problem

A fundamental difference exists between the Oasis shelter program and shelter team (refer to Chapters 8 and 9) and all other programs and teams at the center. The shelter is a 24-hour-a-day, seven-day-a-week operation, while other programs are not continuously in service. The shelter provides temporary food and rest for runaways, for kids who are estranged from their families, and for those who have court-ordered placements. Typically, the residential group of teens is composed of energetic, often emotionally confused youngsters. These children often come to Oasis because other placements could not accommodate their unique emotional needs. In a word, these kids can be a handful. This program is not a babysitting service, however. The shelter provides life skills and academic programming and approaches each child with the intent of helping him or her return to the world as a young person who is better able to cope with internal and external challenges.

Typically, the staff that works at the shelter day and night is composed of people who are trained at a bachelor's degree-level or less. Staff members who work in other programs throughout the Oasis infrastructure tend to be master's degree or doctoral-level professionals. While the rest of Oasis has operated within flexible parameters, the shelter team has had to remain at its posts no matter what. The reasons for these differentials reside in a multiplicity of factors. Chief among them are cost, staff availability, and the nature of the shelter contributions to youth.

The costs associated with hiring teams of staff members who will rotate duties on a 24-hour basis are significantly greater than those that are connected, for example, with hiring several counselors for a program that is limited to an eight-hour day. Finding master's-level and doctoral-level people who are willing to work evening and all-night shifts at the shelter is difficult.

Because the shelter operates in loco parentis with residential youth—many of whom have learned to cope with stress through hostility and acting up—continual vigilance and programming must be the order of the day and night. Such an arrangement often seemed to preclude the possibility that staff could take an hour or two off in order to network, attend meetings, go to training, and so forth. While the reasons for the differences in educational levels and available flexible time between the shelter and most other programs are obvious, however, one of the outcomes associated with those differences was not predicted.

Those at the shelter tended to feel somewhat marginal to the agency. Because their work requires them to be on shelter premises, they have not been able to free themselves for routine and spontaneous meetings at the main offices. Because their educational levels tended to be a bit lower, staff salaries were not quite as high. The outcome was that those at the shelter tended to feel less a part of the overall organization. They have worried that their contributions were less appreciated and that their input was not as valued.

Yet, a refreshing difference exists about the way in which this problem has been handled at Oasis, compared to the way that it might be dealt with in other more traditional organizations. At Oasis, the issue was widely discussed. All aspects of the problem were aired as those who had various perspectives shared their concerns.

Shelter staff members have not kept their issues private, letting them fester into crippling resentments. Rather, those in other parts of the agency have heard the complaints, empathized with them, and have committed the agency to work toward providing solutions. Probably the most striking fact of the person-centered Oasis approach to the issue was that a few years ago, when the problem was most serious, it was not uncommon to hear the issue raised matter-of-fact by people all over the agency. No one seemed to feel the need to sweep the problem under the rug or hide their true feelings about the issue. At the conclusion of the initial data-gathering phase of this research project, the agency had come to grips with this concern. Staff in all parts of the organization had arrived at the conclusion that the problem could no longer be tolerated. Thus, at that point, resolution of this issue had become one of the three priorities that the agency had set for itself.

Inter-Team Communication: Follow-Up   At the conclusion of our study, we found the marginalization of the shelter team largely nonexistent. The change is due, in large part, to the physical completion of the new shelter building but also to personnel efforts and attitudes within the shelter team and among other Oasis associates.

The new shelter facility is approximately one-and-one-half blocks from the main agency building, as opposed to the several miles that separated the previous location. Instead of a 15-minute automobile ride for face-to-face communication, associates can move between these two facilities now with a comfortable five-minute stroll up the street. Most general agency-wide meetings are now held in the shelter. Additionally, the new facility was designed and built with considerable shelter-staff input for maximum functionality. Certainly, the pride factor has had its positive effects, as well. The shelter continued to be a focus of positive community fundraising efforts even after completion of construction, and eventually, the entire mortgage was paid in full.

An Over-Emphasis on Weaknesses

In many parts of the agency, a tendency has existed to focus more heavily on weaknesses than on strengths. While observers all over the city consider this agency to be a jewel and it has won impressive awards at the state and national levels, people within the organization have felt obligated to concentrate on continual improvement strategies. One of their primary tactics has been to keep a sharp eye focused on agency weaknesses, rather than on agency strengths and successes.

Oasis emphasizes the positives and successes of those youth and families who are the object of its intervention efforts. Oasis honors, celebrates, and promotes teens. When it comes to the agency itself, however, it has been more likely to berate than to celebrate. Oasis does occasionally make time available at team meetings for sharing the good things that they have accomplished, but the norm has been to spend more time talking about the failures and errors than the positives during those meetings.

Again, we must remember that this particular agency weakness, like the others, is not so pronounced that it leads to below-average programming. The consequences of this agency characteristic are not disastrous for the center, for the clients, or for the associates themselves. Yet, this characteristic needs to be considered a weakness because it runs counter to the organizational-management model and culture.

Center associates want their attitudes toward themselves to reflect the attitudes that they want their clients to develop toward themselves. When teens focus more intensely on their personal faults, rather than on their strengths, staff members gently assist with refocusing. They believe that youth, like adults, need to emphasize personal positives in order to have resources to fall back on when mistakes are made and when circumstances become difficult. So, this area is one of those rare situations in which the agency, in effect, is asking kids and their families to "do as I say and not as I do." They do not want kids to get hung up on their faults; however, they tolerate that characteristic within the center staff.

Emphasis on the Weaknesses: Follow-Up   At the close of phase one, the agency had been working toward obtaining better balance. Now, it has become increasingly common to hear someone say, "We need to stop beating ourselves up about this. We may not be able to find the solution to this issue right now, but, after all, we wouldn't have this problem if we hadn't been good enough to attract the support that has made this whole program possible in the first place."

Still, during team meetings, far more time is spent on team weaknesses than on accomplishments and strengths. Some voices continue to insist that this situation represents an appropriate balance, because the weaknesses need to be addressed if change is to occur. A substantial number of voices exist, however, that now take the point of view that hearing about gains and successes provides a unique sort of energy to a conversation and makes it possible for others to use effective strategies. In this manner, the "good stuff" becomes embedded within the culture and within the system. Thus, more and more these days, lightening up on the weaknesses in favor of visiting the strengths has come to be a good thing at Oasis.

Relations With the Board

The board of directors and the staff went through some rough times in the 1980s and 1990s. As phase one of the research project came to a close, it was obvious that the center and its board of directors were struggling. A new vision of board-staff relations seemed sorely needed. Some of the more conventional communication patterns between the board and the nonprofit staff were simply not working. Tensions on both sides prompted a serious trip to the drawing board. Everyone hoped that new and more effective roles and methods of operation could be designed and that these new strategies could carry the agency successfully into the 21st century. The importance of this issue for the center and for most nonprofit organizations in contemporary society is so weighty that we devoted Chapter 7 to a thorough discussion of the problems that the center and its board faced and the emerging solutions that began to achieve viability.

SUMMARY: WEAKNESSES

The Oasis weaknesses discussed here were the most noteworthy negatives present at the close of our first data-gathering stage. Thus, these are the weaknesses to which we had longitudinal access. At the initial stages, most people at the agency could articulate well what the problems were, and most had begun to think about solutions. Indeed, we had learned that the Oasis culture did not permit the possibility that a weakness could be discovered, but no remediation was attempted.

Two years into the project, as a research team, we provided perspectives on each of these problems at a meeting of the administrative team, as well as at a general meeting of the entire Oasis staff. Thus, we were keenly aware that most agency personnel shared concern over these issues and that the center had committed itself to address these concerns. A new Oasis executive director had just begun work at that critical point in the agency's history. Relations with the board were in a state of flux.

As you are now aware, the longitudinal information we provide here was based on cyclical revisiting of these issues across time. As we returned for data gathering, our focus was on the hypotheses that were formed subsequent to the early stage of inquiry. In several important ways, however, the agency had changed across time—and we were required to form new hypotheses about increasingly important organizational dynamics. In general, these significant changes were programmatic in nature. At the close of the five-year project, we discovered no new weaknesses that were substantial enough to report. As we shared regarding the issue of weaknesses, the situation seemed to be that the organization tended to be repeating its mistakes in a couple of noteworthy areas.

The new factors that we did note across time tended to be in areas that were previously not relevant, and it is most accurate to think of these programmatic dynamics as strengths, rather than weaknesses. In fact, the Oasis person-centered model seemed to hold up rather well across time. We will discuss the issues of programmatic change and the robustness of the management model at the close of this chapter.

STRENGTHS AND OUTCOMES

In Chapter 5, "The Oasis Person-Centered Model," we outlined the Oasis person-centered approach to leadership and management. Throughout our descriptions of how this agency is run, we have made references to the impact that these leadership strategies have on staff, clients, and programming. Having moved through the previous chapters, the reader at this point already has a substantial introduction to this organization's strengths. Our focus here shifts from an emphasis on person-centered management strategies to an emphasis on outcomes and results that are the products of person-centered processes. We will summarize each of the most potent ones and provide a vignette that illustrates the point. Within this agency, the most noteworthy outcomes that can be attributed to person-centered participatory management are as follows:

1. Teens and family clients replace dysfunctional coping mechanisms with positive attitudes and behaviors that contribute to healthy development. Oasis clients get better.

2. The agency has a well-developed capability to respond quickly to community needs through the development of outstanding creative programs.

3. Locally and nationally, the agency enjoys a superior reputation for community service.

4. Agency professionals do not experience the burnout that is typically associated with staff members in similar kinds of nonprofit positions elsewhere.

Teens and Families Get Better

On a hot southern summer afternoon, we visited at length in the home of a mother whose family's history with Oasis is representative of the agency's clientele. This 30-something-year-old woman (we will call her Norma) had an important story to tell. One of the first things that she wanted us to know was that as a result of her work with one of the Oasis counselors (we will call her Ruth), she was now able to tell her story. Prior to her work at Oasis, she had not had any coherent understanding of who she was or how her experiences had helped to form her attitudes and her life.

Both of Norma's parents had been alcoholics, and she has an extensive history as a casualty within a pattern of abuse. She had been the victim of childhood sexual abuse. As a young adult, she married—and subsequently divorced—two physically abusive husbands. When her eldest child, a girl, reached her teen years, she began to physically abuse her mother in response to family frustrations. During volatile periods with her ex-husbands, guns and gunfire terrorized her and her children.

As a teen, Norma had dropped out of high school—and, as a result, she had drifted from one low-paying job to another. Within the years prior to forming a relationship with Oasis, Norma had lost employment and went into bankruptcy. Because of an inability to manage her family as a single parent, she endured the pain of temporary loss of the youngest of her four children, who was placed into a foster home by the Department of Health and Human Services.

Norma's coping mechanisms ran a range that included lies, alcohol, and affairs with married men. Norma described herself as a person who had made a habit of being a "complete liar." She told us that she had not really made much of a distinction between truth and falsehood throughout most of her upbringing and early adulthood.

Her first contact with Oasis occurred when the courts referred her eldest daughter to one of the center programs. Norma began seeing Ruth, an Oasis counselor, and as the relationship between the two formed, she told us that it became the healthiest relationship she had ever experienced. "Because of her, I feel like now I'm a real person," Norma says. "I feel good about myself. I have self-confidence. Ruth taught me that I can communicate."

The family's relationship with the center has been extensive. The eldest daughter was a resident at the shelter for a while. She and a younger brother participated in one of the after-school life skills programs that the center runs on school property. One of the other children met with another member of the Oasis counseling team for six months. During a lean Christmastime, the center provided Norma's family with much-needed food and gave her "money to buy Christmas stuff, even when the churches wouldn't," Norma says. Despite the family's successful use of a variety of Oasis services, Norma's counseling relationship with Ruth has remained the core of the family's connection with Oasis. "Ruth inspires me," Norma says. "No matter what has gone wrong, she says, 'We'll work this out.' And we always do. I was at the point of putting a gun to my head when I came here. Now, I'm a happy person who mostly knows how to do what needs to be done."

Norma cited many examples of her new-found skills. One of them she particularly appreciates is something she and her counselor call "timeout." Norma says that she has learned that emotional crises among her and the kids do not have to be responded to right that minute. They now follow their family rule that when emotions run high, they stop trying to work on the problem. After a reflective period, when tempers and frustrations have cooled, they come back to the problem, knowing that volatility has been avoided and that they will likely now find at least a temporary resolution. "It's just a miracle that one of us didn't kill one another before—especially when the guns were in the house," Norma says. "This is just so much different now, and so much better!" In fact, Norma currently has a good-paying job and is taking classes to obtain her *General Equivalency Diploma* (GED). She has been living for quite some time with a "good man, a communicator," who is not an abusive partner and who accompanies her to premarital sessions at Oasis in order to increase their ability to talk meaningfully with one another.

Ruth says that over the course of their two-year counseling relationship, she has watched Norma evolve into an involved and concerned mother. "She was a woman full of shame with many of the typical thought processes that we associate with battered women," Ruth says. "For example, when one of the kids did something wrong, she'd assume that it might really be her fault, so she'd let them off. She hadn't realized that she had strengths and wisdom within herself." At one point, Ruth became aware that her client had waved a gun at the children out of frustration and an inability to cope. "Now, she fully realizes what a huge mistake that was and she has many strategies to use in place of that dysfunctional one," Ruth says.

"Norma uses this as a place of advice for parenting, for learning about life, and for healing as a woman," Ruth says. "I admire and respect her. She didn't quit. I'm in awe of the changes in spite of the odds." As is the case with other successful clients—both teens and parents—Norma eventually became involved as an enabler at the center in addition to her role as services consumer. She has co-led Oasis groups for troubled parents and has spoken about effective parenting in community forums outside the Oasis building.

Teamwork, creativity, and the core Oasis culture paid off for Norma and her family. Because the counseling relationship between Norma and Ruth formed the core of the family's alliance with the agency, the Counseling Team, through Ruth, assumed responsibility for coordinating agency efforts on behalf of this family. The team approach enabled the agency to provide a coherent set of services so that the right hand always knew what the left hand was doing.

The Oasis person-centered concept that might have made the biggest difference was the agency's investment in the development of its staff. Ruth says that the agency's respect for her, and its insistence that she take care of herself, led her to offer these same things to her client. "I wanted for Norma what I have been given here—the opportunity to come from the heart, to be direct, to celebrate the spirituality and the godliness that happens when people can hear and people can speak," Ruth says. She says that Oasis looks for the best in her, and she in turn looks for the best in her clients.

A Stellar National and Local Reputation

Oasis has won many awards that could legitimately be the envy of any number of nonprofit organizations. Appropriately, these accolades salute both programs and people. In 1999, Oasis won the Not-for-Profit Award from the National Conference for Community and Justice. The *Teen Outreach Program* (TOP) was the 1998 Southeastern Network's Model Program Award, and in 1999, the Second Harvest Food Bank saluted both the TOP and Nashville Youth PULSE. In 1994, the Family Retreat Weekend received the Southeastern Network Program Award, while the Peer Educator Program was the *Hospital Corporation of America* (HCA) Award of Achievement for Volunteer Excellence recipient.

People are behind the programs, of course. In 1998, Deanna Scales, director of support services, was a finalist for the Council of Community Service Unsung Hero Award, and Kristina Treanor, board of directors youth representative and peer educator, was listed among Radio Shack's 200 of the Brightest, Most Industrious Minds in America. The previous year, Ronnie Wenzler, board president, and Sherry Allen, associate executive director, were saluted by the Southeastern Network of Youth as Outstanding Board Member and TAPP Middle Manager Award recipient, respectively.

Creating Good Programs Quickly

Oasis associates try to listen as closely to the community as they do to their clients and to one another. When they hear of a pressing need or a particularly entrenched societal problem, they become interested. They want to help, and they believe they can. The agency can become up to speed in understanding a problem in a relatively short time. They can design a responsive program in an equally brief period. As soon as a program gets off the ground, evaluation efforts are begun so that weaknesses that are inherent in the design can be quickly addressed. As one observer put it, "Oasis has the ability to create quickly and the ability to profit quickly from mistakes."

One such program is *People United, Leading, and Serving Everywhere* (PULSE). Described in more detail in the next section, PULSE saw a need for youth to make a positive volunteer impact on the community, brought adult and youth resources together quickly, and made success happen. Part of its success includes reflection forms for volunteers, providing PULSE instant feedback on what worked well and what did not.

Commitment to the Individual Associate

Program Development

Typically, we have considered the development of individuals and agency programs as two separate factors. Julie Falender's story, however, powerfully illustrates that these two strengths are still present at Oasis. This story also shows how, within this organization, these two have complemented one another over the years. Additionally, Falender's involvement at Oasis is a strong example of the new youth-leadership mission in action. As Executive Director Ronnie Steine notes, "We have for too long done things *for* young people and done things *to* young people. Now it's time to do things *with* young people. We need to focus on youth participation and youth/adult partnerships."

Falender first came to Oasis as a high school freshman volunteer, following in the footsteps of her older sister Allison, who served as a peer educator. Falender participated in the first two ASB programs, first in South Dakota on a Sioux Indian reservation and second with an inner-city church in Rochester, New York. Rather than basking at the beach during spring break, Falender and other volunteers, along with their Oasis leaders, cleaned up the Indian community center, worked with kids after school, and heightened awareness of addiction prevalence. The second year, they worked in a halfway house, church daycare, a thrift shop—anything that needed to be done.

Falender is quick to emphasize the value of these experiences, which are so different from her own growing up in a stable family, attending a private school kindergarten through eighth grade, and being active in her synagogue. Falender's true challenge, however, occurred the summer before her junior year in high school. She was traveling abroad that summer and received an e-mail from Oasis. There was a new part-time staff position, Youth Volunteer Assistant, and would she like to apply? "I debated about applying," states Falender frankly. "I was playing basketball and taking *Advanced Placement* (AP) classes. I'd have to give up the team to take the job."

Indeed, she did come to work for Oasis. After the standard Oasis team interview, including four or five staff associates and another youth volunteer, Falender became the first paid youth staff member. She joined the *Youth Leadership Development* (YLD) Team under the direction of Jane Fleishman. The YLD team was developing a new program, PULSE. PULSE is a cooperative effort between Oasis, Hands-On Nashville, and the Frist Foundation, which is designed to partner youth and adults in volunteer projects throughout the city. Falender started with 30 youth volunteers and four projects. Now two years old, PULSE involves more than 500 youth who are recruited through schools and churches. Monthly calendars offer volunteer opportunities during the week and on weekends that diversely target kids up to the elderly. Volunteers can easily find projects that are tailored to their particular interests. Annually, there is a PULSE day in April that is the culmination of these year-long efforts. The first year, PULSE Day attracted 330 youth and adults for a day of volunteerism. The second April captured more than 700. As one 14-year old who was working to clean up a neighborhood playground noted, "It doesn't pay in the pocket; it pays in the heart."

Steine notes that "Our young people are at worst devalued and at best undervalued. Increasingly, adults fear teens and are uncomfortable or uneasy in their presence. Our perceptions are fueled by the media that treats teens the same way they deal with general news: the focus is on the worst, the most sensational and aberrational of behaviors and activities." Falender and PULSE are marvelous examples that this situation is just not so.

Not only did Falender help launch PULSE, but she also notes her own personal growth, as well. Falender reports that "everyone embraced me" at Oasis. "People at Oasis are very accepting; in touch with the community and themselves," she says. Falender describes co-workers as a "loving family; the most amazing people in Nashville."

Falender was not just nurtured and supported in her job; we might ascribe that to her newness and youth. Like other Oasis associates, Falender was challenged to stretch. "They looked at my skills and pushed me—nudged me along," she says. Falender cites being invited to give ideas to other agency program teams, participating in multiple hiring interviews, and performing stints on television talk shows and with civic groups. Falender is a member of the newly-formed Mayor's Youth Advisory Council, which was instituted at Falender's suggestion. She works with the director of Metro Parks to provide drug-free teen band performances through the parks system. She has attended conferences in Washington, D.C. and has led training sessions in Georgia.

Falender has now graduated from high school (with a substantial Oasis contingency in attendance at her graduation) and plans to study public policy and sociology at Brown University. Did her work at Oasis steer her in this direction? "I am the person I am because of Oasis," she says. "If I ever do anything amazing, I owe it all to them."

Oasis staff are quick to reverse the credit, however. At Falender's farewell staff party, Steine summed up the situation well: "When we started all this a couple, three years ago and we all sort of dreamed about involving young people on staff here, we could never have imagined that one could join us and have such an immediate impact and help us literally set the standard for what we hope to continue to do in the future," he says.

Yes, having met Falender, we are confident that she is an exceptional young person. The organization seems to have pulled her best from her, however, and the attitude of "you've helped me; no you've helped me more" is an Oasis cultural benchmark.

Here, we have program development and personal development, working in tandem with one another in a person-centered environment. PULSE has Falender largely to thank for its strong format and quick growth, and Falender has grown and matured in the Oasis way. Both are richer for the experience.

Clearly, the management structures within Oasis still give more attention to the staff member than to the client, believing that staff members who are treated well and are encouraged to grow will treat clients well, encouraging the same sort of growth. This dynamic relationship has significantly reduced burnout and has greatly improved, by all reports, the personal lives of staff and clients (as well as the development of stellar programmatic efforts).

A Burnout-Free Environment

As a previous chapter revealed, burnout in the social-service professions is an issue of staggering proportions. Service providers leave agencies and leave the field. Of equal concern, however, are the great numbers of people who remain in their social-service positions but have functionally disengaged from their work and clients due to the emotional stresses associated with burnout. One of the greatest strengths of the Oasis management program is that it results in a significant reduction or even elimination of burnout syndrome.

Oasis associates are creative in fitting the person to the task. Denise Becker takes a break from her counseling role to take on facilities maintenance, for example. "I just love the chance to do something concrete, like minor repairs that are immediately visible," she says. Becker's "minor maintenance work" extends to major telephone-system upgrades and the implementation of a new computer system.

Deanna Scales cites creative job retooling for helping avoid burnout. When Oasis was able to hire additional receptionist support, Scales redefined Mindy Hunter's role to include her love of shopping. Now, Hunter not only staffs the busy receptionist desk, but she uses her natural shopping savvy to get competitive bids and great deals on all kinds of supplies for the agency. "Mindy has taken on a whole new persona!" exclaims Scales.

Possibly, the reduction of burnout among Oasis employees is one of the most important results of person-centered leadership. When smart, talented people are able to give their all to their jobs and careers—while maintaining satisfying personal lives—clients have a far better chance to reap the rewards of their social-service efforts.

SUMMARY: STRENGTHS AND OUTCOMES

The four strengths we cite here are certainly not the only positive results to which we could have directed attention. As prior pages (and those yet to come) reveal, many areas of noteworthy achievement exist for which this organization has become well known—and to which Oasis points when asked about its management style. We chose to talk about these four achievements: client functioning, a quick response to community needs, a stellar reputation, and individual development and significantly reduced burnout. These accomplishments are bread-and-butter issues in nonprofit venues today.

Organizations want to assist with client well-being in a way that responds to the unique community concerns that they encounter. They also need to accomplish this task in such a way that does not result in stress and harm to staff professionals. Their efforts need to engender public recognition—the kind of response that gains increased funding and makes people feel good about their contributions to their jobs and communities. Oasis has been demonstrating that its person-centered approach to management can provide the agency with the opportunities it needs to accomplish these critical nonprofit goals.

A NOTE ON LEADERSHIP VERSUS MANAGEMENT

Oasis has taken the approach that we present in Chapter 3 regarding a consideration of differences between organizational leadership and management. Theirs is a person-centered approach that represents what is typically the case in person-centered organizations: associates at all levels are expected to perform leadership functions and management functions. Leadership at Oasis involves skills in vision-spinning and inspiration. People expect one another to design a future and to co-create that future. They believe that providing motivation and inspiration to each other is simply part of everybody's job description. At the same time, individuals are expected to be good managers. The skills that they want to claim include planning, facilitating, implementing, and following through. When you hear people use the term *management* at this person-centered agency, they are typically referring to leadership functions *and* management functions—as is the case in other types of person-centered organizations. Within a person-centered model, a management system necessarily demands leadership skills and functions.

A VIEW OF THE ROBUSTNESS OF THE MODEL

Our longitudinal approach revealed that the model we described in the previous chapter was functioning as well at the close of the five-year project as it was at the beginning. We arrive at this conclusion after considering longitudinal data that relate to the following questions:

- Are each of the components that we originally identified still substantially in place?
- Are there competing components that reflect a different leadership philosophy and set of strategies?
- Do the majority of staffers continue to cite the management model as the reason for agency outcomes and successes?

Our answers to these questions are "Yes," "No," and "Yes," respectively. Thus we conclude that the person-centered leadership and management model that we described permeates the organization now, just as it did in the 1990s. In fact, the struggle with—and resolution of—the board-staff discomforts that you will read about in the next chapter provided an opportunity for the organization to take stock consciously of its leadership philosophy and management strategies. As a result, at the beginning of this 21st century, most people in the organization are better able to articulate the model than they once were. Associates in all parts of the organization had the opportunity to reaffirm their commitment to the model. Suggesting that this reaffirmation and increased ability to talk about the specifics of the management model and its consequences for the organization seems fair and might well mean that the model is evenly more thoroughly embedded than it was some years ago.

In the following three chapters, you will learn about specific ways in which the model is implemented and will gain more detailed information about the outcomes that it engenders. In a final chapter, we talk about new programs that are emerging and how the agency has positioned itself for service in this new century.

REFERENCE

Deal, T. E. and Kennedy, A. A. (1982). *Corporate cultures: The rites and rituals of corporate life*. Reading, MA: Addison-Wesley.

7

The Board of Directors
The Creation of a
New Participatory Model

On a warm—and what turned out to be interesting—October evening, we had our first formal contact with the Oasis board. We had been heavily into this research project for approximately six months, and at that point, we had a reasonably firm grasp of the infrastructure, culture, and operations of the agency—as well as its place in the community. While we had learned about the board's functions from the agency-personnel point of view, however, we had interviewed by that time only a single board member. Thus, in the category of dynamics between the organization and its board, we had only half the picture. We needed an understanding of those dynamics from the board point of view.

THE STAFF POINT OF VIEW

Agency staff of all types had given us a rather uniform message about this board. They knew the 22 board members to be energetic, enthusiastic, and people who represented diverse corners of the community. The work of these board members (with Oasis and other organizations) had not been oriented exclusively toward raising funds or personally donating money. Rather, they had a reputation for hands-on involvement in their service work. People told us about the board's exemplary public relations activities.

For example, a board member had recently been responsible for a series of articles concerning innovative teen-aged programs through Atlantic Records. Despite staff enthusiasm about individual board members, however, our interviews tended to yield comments that reflected a generalized uneasiness about the board's functioning.

Often, we heard associates worry out loud about staff representation on the board. The executive director attended all board meetings, of course, and had become the main conduit of information. Occasionally, members of the Management Team went to the Tuesday night board meetings. A professional working in another agency commented on the relative infrequency of staff member-board member contact, saying that this part of Oasis's functioning seemed inconsistent with its culture. She pointed out that the traditional model of board-agency relations dictated that there should not be board member contact with staff. Conventional wisdom has held that information must travel back and forth through the director. In that way, staff presumably is protected from "meddling" board members, while the latter are protected from getting individual requests for donations and from the possibility of misinterpreting the agency's mission or position through false information that a single staff member might relate. Our outside informant shared her puzzlement that a participatory agency such as Oasis would function in such a conventional way with a relatively traditional, non-participatory board. Her concerns were echoed by many in the agency who said that they wished more staff members could attend board meetings. They hoped that there could come a time when board members frequently visited the agency to observe, participate, and help create programming.

Several associates mentioned that it was inconsistent with Oasis philosophy and culture to have such a sizable, influential group that did not have "teen representation on it." Two individuals even worried that the board might be a "rubber-stamp board" that was so impressed with the agency and its director that it simply did not question proposals. While those voices were not joined by a multitude of others, a clear sense of confusion existed about what the board was up to from time to time. One staffer who was particularly concerned said that clearly, a problematic distance existed between the board and the agency. She described this situation as "a sense of the board as 'Other.'" Another staff associate talked about the Oasis cultural mandate that all people must accept. As she applied this concept to board relations, it meant for her that staff members should give the same acceptance to the board that they give to teens, families, and one another—and that the board should offer that sort of acceptance to agency personnel. As she thought about the tensions and possible areas of disagreement, she commented, "But, it's not easy. We're all strong, educated people. Many of us feel we're right. We're still learning to accept this part of our journey, to learn through these difficulties."

In general, we found uniform opinion about the board and its relationship with staff members. People spoke highly of individual members and their achievements, were impressed with the commitment and enthusiasm of most board members, and saw the fruits of the board's efforts—both within the agency and within the community. Weaknesses seemed to lie in the communications areas. Not enough communication existed to satisfy most associates. In the absence of staff-board dialogue, many tended to think of the board as something that existed apart from Oasis. Board actions were questioned and/or misunderstood. Occasionally, an uncomfortable amount of suspicion about the board's attitudes would surface. To many employees, it seemed clear that Oasis personnel did not think of the board as a partner in their social-service mission. Thinking of the board as "Other" was ubiquitous at Oasis.

A BOARD MEETING TO REMEMBER

We were asked to attend that early autumn board meeting in order to present the results of our initial investigation of Oasis culture, methods, and standing in the community. Because our inquiries had resulted in such positive information about this innovative nonprofit organization, we were particularly happy to oblige. Indeed, our data had revealed this agency to be so outstanding that we found ourselves looking forward to the opportunity to share good news with this hard-working board.

We reviewed agency weaknesses for the board but spent more time on Oasis strengths, because the positives far outweighed the negatives. After an overview of data related to the successes that emerge from the Oasis culture, we let them know that we had told members of the Management Team that we were also going to share some information and concerns about current staff-board functioning. These remarks would reflect the staff point of view, of course, because we had not yet launched a full investigation of board-member perspectives.

We began by sharing positive attitudes that we heard time and time again about individual board members and the enthusiastic work of the board in public relations activities around town. Then, we moved to a presentation of the single area of concern: communication. We talked briefly about the staff's desire to be more involved at board meetings and to encourage board participation at the agency program sites. Overall, our initial overview of staff-board dynamics did not exceed about 10 minutes. Because of its brevity and because we had not yet had in-depth interviews with a number of board members, we were almost completely unprepared for the reaction that our remarks precipitated.

Board members immediately began to voice frustration. Several started talking at once. Most of the board members at this meeting had a fairly strong—and concerned—reaction to the idea that there were communication problems between staff and board members. A few minutes were necessary to sort things out, but soon a message came through loud and clear: Any communication problems that might exist were co-created by the staff as well as by the board. Several indicated that the board had never said that staff members should not attend the monthly meetings. One said that those associates who had attended meetings often did not contribute. This person noted that from time to time, the associates seemed peeved rather than participatory. Another commented that there had been times when she and another board member had talked about visiting the agency—or had expressed the desire to participate in programming—only to be told that "wasn't such a good idea right now." After 20 minutes or so of hearing reactions, we clearly realized that this committed and enthusiastic board had been feeling many of the same things that staff members had been reporting. In essence, they had felt left out of things. Their participation in agency functioning seemed equally as unwelcome as staff felt their participation in board activities might be.

Eventually, a member who had held an Oasis board position for quite some time began to reminisce about the early days of the agency. "In those days, we all had picnic suppers together—board and staff," she said. She talked about the ease with which communication flowed between staff and board some 10 to 15 years ago when the agency was still in its infancy. "I miss those days," she said. "In fact, I feel cheated that those opportunities are not offered anymore."

One of the members seated toward the rear of the room prompted a rather thorough discussion of "staff's unwillingness to tell us about specific cases." People noted that associates were ethical, responsible people who went to great lengths to protect confidentiality. "The problem is that we end up not knowing the success stories," said one rather frustrated individual. "And the community doesn't hear much about them either. How can we develop an adequate funding campaign if we can't inform people about the excellence of the product?" Another person said, "I think they go too far trying to protect the kids' identities. They could change the names or some facts in the story, and we (and others) would never be able to guess who was involved. Yet, we would share the feelings of success. Our own enthusiasm would grow and be contagious." All present seemed to think that this issue directly affected fundraising potentials.

At one point, an image emerged of Oasis being currently in an adolescent stage of development. This idea seemed to fit for several of those who were in attendance that evening. After all, the agency had grown so fast and with so many options, successes, and so much energy that it seemed reasonable to think about the agency as an organization on its way to maturity. As they bounced around this image, some board members found comfort in the idea that the current staff might be experiencing an adolescence of sorts and felt that the board needed to function in the more traditional parental roles. Yet, this image was disturbing to others who saw it as a possibility for more distance between board and staff. One person conjectured, "While we need different roles, there needs to be participation of mature equals—some with service functions (the staff) and others with legal and guidance functions (the board)."

Most members talked about their willingness to get involved with teens and staff despite busy personal and professional schedules. One person remarked, "If they just would have asked, I would have found some time." Clearly, this board felt a personal fondness and commitment for this agency that would be seen as enviable in other nonprofit organizations throughout the country. Yet, they—like their staff counterparts—also felt disenfranchised to some extent. They functioned as responsible overseers but felt a separation from the agency that somehow did not fit with what they understood Oasis to be.

By the close of this conversation, most people were echoing a point of view that recognized that Oasis was such a successfully innovative nonprofit organization that its board needed to learn to chart new territory, too. These individuals wanted to co-create with the staff more useful and creative ways of relating and communicating. Several expressed a desire to work more closely with teens as well as staff. Everyone seemed committed to entering a new phase of dialogue—although it was unclear at that point just exactly where a new sort of staff-board partnership might lead.

Follow-Through

When we and the board members conveyed the dynamics and dialogue of this meeting to the Oasis staff and to the Management Team, a flutter of defensiveness emerged. This situation was extremely short-lived, however.

Quickly, people on both sides—board and staff—mobilized for action and change. Following a session in which we processed these issues with the Management Team, Judy Freudenthal, Counseling Team director, wrote a letter of commitment to the board president. The letter read, in part:

> Today, Dr. Jeanne Plas and Sue Lewis shared observations and perceptions that serve to better inform us as we continue through this transition period. It was a powerful experience to hear both the strengths and weaknesses of Oasis. I feel equally committed to sustaining the strengths, and addressing the weaknesses. I regret anything I have done, or not done, that may have contributed to a breakdown in communication with the Board. I assure you there is an eagerness to proceed together with the Board and new Executive Director in staking out our continued (and corrected) path towards excellence.
>
> Thank you for investing yourself in us, and the youth and families we serve. It appears we have a remarkable ability to make a difference in the lives of the people we serve—as well as our own. I, and the rest, look forward to working together with the Board in further establishing Oasis as a treasure of an agency.

Small groups of board and staff members set themselves the task of developing ideas for change. One of the first ideas that took root was a shadowing plan. Quite quickly, however, the basic idea was altered. Instead of assigning a board member to shadow a staff member for a while, people decided that they wanted a board member and staff member to team up, identifying projects and roles from different but equal vantage points. The dyads scheduled themselves for time on the board member's professional turf, as well as within Oasis programs. All across the agency, dialogue began to spring up as board members telephoned staff and staff invited board members to planning sessions.

As we finished the core phase of our investigation, no roles, functions, or communication paths or patterns had been officially or unofficially developed.

Relations between agency personnel and the board of directors were in flux. All seemed to agree, however, that "very good things were happening" and that a new era of board-staff partnership undoubtedly had begun. We turn now to a description of what transpired between these two entities over the next few years.

COMMUNICATION PATTERNS

When we reviewed the data that we had collected concerning board-staff relations, we had to inevitably conclude that a substantial amount of friction existed. When we categorized the issues, we learned that most concerns resulted from a lack of communication between the board and staff. In fact, as is typical in many nonprofit organizations, few channels for communication existed between the board and staff members. Because this agency is not a typical nonprofit organization, those who are on the staff, the board, and within the community had noted with various degrees of concern that it might be wise to redefine and rework board functioning and relationships with the staff if the center's unique goals were to be realized. As we disengaged from that initial stage of the project, many on both sides of the table were paying at least lip service to the idea that change had to occur in this set of dynamics if Oasis was to continue to develop its potential. Yet, a redefinition of the relationship between the board and the nonprofit agency is a daunting task at best, given the role of the board as overseer and the levels of board-staff distrust that are often almost institutionalized around the country within these settings.

Conventional Board-Staff Dynamics

The factors involved in typical board-staff relations are well known. Board members are typically unpaid citizens who volunteer out of a sense of social responsibility or because their corporate organizations have asked them to participate in community work of some sort. These people usually take service time out of their personal lives, rather than their work lives. Often, people believe that board members bring to the table areas of expertise that are not found among nonprofit personnel; specifically, skills in the area of fiscal management and responsibility. Thus, a paternal (or at least, avuncular) relationship often develops between the two constituencies, with board members ultimately responsible (by law and presumed higher levels of interest) for financial matters, including staff salaries.

The Role of the Executive Director

Further complicating the situation is a tacit understanding that a major portion of the executive director's job is to be the conduit of information between board and staff. Assumedly, staff members might pester board members with requests for donations and so forth if they had direct access. Board members might develop negative views of staff functioning if they were to observe isolated bits of staff behavior while on site. Furthermore, they might start suggesting treatment plans, although they are bereft of the expertise required for that sort of decision-making. Thus, conventional wisdom has held that these two groups should acknowledge one another's special areas of expertise and leave the executive director to negotiate the middle ground. Obviously, this sort of situation institutionalizes a certain amount of fear, and it makes it impossible for both sides to reap the benefits of the other's knowledge bases and good will.

The Oasis Approach to the Problem

After reviewing the issues just mentioned, we realized that Oasis was taking on a gargantuan task in its desire to reform board-staff relationships. Yet, along with others in the community, it also seemed to us that the Oasis management project could not hope to truly succeed in the long run if this feat were not accomplished. So, we are particularly pleased to report that this part of the commitment package that Oasis adopted in the '90s has been realized—to a great extent beyond the dreams and expectations of those who participated and those of us who observed.

The first event that happened was an airing of concerns, differences, suspicions, and expectations. This discussion occurred primarily at a few board meetings, but it also importantly occurred in dyadic and small-group telephone and face-to-face conversations. Those on both sides of the table began to pick up the telephone to ask a question and/or to offer a suggestion or invitation. As we mentioned in a previous chapter, they seized the common idea of shadowing right away. This group made the decision that board members should shadow staff members and staff members should shadow board members, however. This system proved to be a remarkably effective strategy for beginning the dialogue that eventually caused all of the changes to occur.

As of this writing, we are not exaggerating when we say that the dynamics governing board-staff relations are completely different now than they were in the previous century. Now, staff members of all sorts regularly attend board meetings and contribute substantially. Recognizing the need for two-way input prompted everyone to realize that the youth voice had been missing. So, teen members of the board are now a vital reality.

Keys to Problem Resolution

One of the major keys to the current relationship are work groups—teams that develop policy and guide operations. Each of these groups—fundraising, program development, and so forth—contains staff as well as board members.

A second key is lodged within communication expectations. Not only is cross-talk between these two constituencies tolerated, but it is also mandated. People call one another fairly frequently. Board members are well aware of daily struggles and successes at the agency. As an example, consider a recent difficulty with a staff member's fiscal responsibilities and performance. In the past, this agency—like other nonprofit groups—would have handled the problem in house, deciding that staff was solely responsible for dealing with this sort of thing and feeling some reluctance to air dirty linen with board members who might get a biased view of staff competencies and responsibility quotients. Now, however, the organization does not operate from this sort of fear mindset. In this instance, at least three staff members were on the phone to board members within hours of the problem coming to light. If asked about this specific difficulty now, staff members at the center would be quick to tell you that the board's role was invaluable in assessing the problem and developing creative and responsible ways of dealing with the situation. "Board members were with us every step of the way," says Deanna Scales, Office Services director. "Board members brought specific and helpful ideas. It was great not to be out there by ourselves. Nothing was hidden under the rug."

THE FUTURE

By all accounts, this agency has a stellar board-staff partnership that can serve as a model for any agency that recognizes that more traditional ways of running nonprofit organizations might not be capable of responding to the demands of this new century. We noted that one of the more exciting prospects for the center these days centers on the opportunities to offer consultation concerning board-staff relationships to other organizations who are experiencing the sort of pain that Oasis once did as a result of deteriorated communication and trust levels between the staff and board.

Strategies for Practice: Creating a Participatory Board

1. Organize a focus group to begin discussion about this new strategy. Be sure that the group is representative of both new and more established board members and staff associates from all levels of the organization.

2. Be explicit in focus-group meetings about the nature of the proposed change and its potential impact on agency functioning, as well as role changes for all players involved.

   Caution: Most nonprofit organizations tend to be either staff-driven or board-driven. That is, one group tends to dominate functions that direct the work of the agency. Logically, nonprofit organizations that have small staffs tend to be more board-driven, while larger organizations with substantial staff associates do more of the work. This approach is *not* either-or; rather, it incorporates a balance of both sides into the communication loops.

3. Invite focus-group members to go back to their respective constituents and receive feedback on these ideas.

4. Repeat the focus group-feedback cycle until the issue is clearly on the table.

5. Conduct a retreat with full board and staff participation so that concepts and feedback can be summarized and discussed more fully.

6. Brainstorm new ways of communicating that enable fuller board-staff interactions. Possibilities include shadowing or partnering board and staff members at both of their respective work sites and direct cross-talk with staff sharing program updates at board meetings and board representatives relaying current board activities at periodic staff meetings.

7. Implement new communication strategies experimentally, being alert to feedback as to what does and does not work. Use the original focus group in a possible monitoring role.

8. As the new participatory style becomes established, use this technique explicitly in the recruitment of new board members and staff associates. Most people will find the model quite different from their experiences in other organizations.

9. Incorporate these strategies into the orientation and training programs for new staff and board members. Again, people need to understand the differences and be a part of them.

10. Consider periodic events that enhance direct communication, such as annual retreats, informal social gatherings, or personal profiling of individuals to help make getting acquainted easier.

8

The Shelter
Against All Odds

In Chapter 4, "Oasis Center: An Overview," we introduced the shelter as a 24-hour residential facility where youth can stay as a refuge from homelessness, domestic violence, exposure to abusive substances, or other crises. While at the shelter, residents continue in an educational program that is recognized by the Metro school system, a structured living program, and individual and group counseling in order to gain survival and living skills as well as to address individual and family issues. Youth who come to the shelter often feel deep despair and hopelessness.

CHALLENGING CIRCUMSTANCES

If it is true that physical surroundings have a lot to do with a positive work environment, then the entire shelter program staff should have been clinically depressed. Three months before we began our research at Oasis, a fire completely gutted the shelter building that stood next to the main agency building. That heart-breaking fire destroyed or badly damaged supplies, records, furniture, personal items, and a good bit of staff morale. Yet, there were positives about the fire: no one was seriously injured, and the adjacent administrative building was unharmed. Community and even regional support was immediate and substantial. Just a few hours after the fire, country music singer Trisha Yearwood walked in the front door to ask how she could help. Two shelter programs in other states held fundraisers for Oasis. Parents of past shelter clients offered financial aid and other material support. Despite the abundant community outpouring, however, the fire was internally a tremendous stressor that took its toll on more than just wood, brick, and mortar.

Staff flew immediately into crisis mode, both to make arrangements for displaced youth and to handle the barrage of media attention that the fire created. They had to carve a niche in the already-bustling main agency building while alternate facilities could be located. Kids who could not be placed elsewhere temporarily slept on agency couches while overnight staff maintained vigil. Day shelter staff began to feel as if they were getting in the way of other agency employees. For example, the shelter staff planned a graduation ceremony and party for 10 kids who had earned their *General Equivalency Diplomas* (GEDs). Assuming that all agency staff members were equally as thrilled at the youths' successful milestone, shelter employees busied themselves decorating the agency building with balloons and planning the details of the event. Tensions tightened when someone suggested that they were taking over the building while other agency teams had to proceed with scheduled programs as well.

After six weeks, the shelter program located alternate accommodations in a Metro Davidson county residential facility know as The Village. Here, the shelter team began to work and maintain its 24-hour, 365-day-a-year open house to adolescents 13 to 17 years of age who were in crisis resulting from suicide attempts, family estrangement, substance abuse, or gang involvement. The shelter program resided at The Village during the entire first year of our research as funds were raised and a new shelter facility was built. This location was temporary and terrible.

The building was dated, had never been renovated, and had that beige feel of worn-out institutionalism. The linoleum had yellowed and cracked, and although it was mopped daily, it always had a grungy look. Perhaps that is why the lights in the hallways and rooms always seemed dim and dreary. The youth shared crowded bedrooms with even smaller baths and used one community laundry room that was always overflowing with baskets of dirty clothes waiting in turn for their owners to have an appointed laundry time. All of the furniture was worn out, colorless, and mismatched. We would have understood if the frumpy, second-hand couches had symbolized the mood of the staff—yet, they certainly did not.

While there were a few rooms in the back that provided limited private office space, the hub of program operations flowed from the crowded

6-by-8-foot cubicle of a front office. There, staff maintained its 24-hour protective surveillance of the resident youth; and often, surly adolescents frequently challenged program rules and staff authority.

Chris, a young man who had suffered child neglect, had been deserted by his mother. Suffering from acute tooth decay, Chris was at the shelter because the grandmother with whom he had been living was suffering from advanced stages of cancer, and alternate living arrangements were being sought. Chris displayed lots of anger, labeled himself as bad, and tested limits all of the time. On one occasion, Chris made a water balloon from a condom and traveled through the shelter, threatening to bomb it. Shelter counselor Frances Rich was seen walking calmly behind Chris with a trash can, encouraging him to properly dispose of the unusual water balloon, stating that she was confident he would do the right thing and reminding him of standard shelter consequences should he decide not to oblige. Suddenly, Chris whirled about to face Frances, holding the water balloon menacingly back as if to throw it, while Frances calmly waited with cool assurance—holding the invitational trash can in front of her. After a few tense seconds, Chris lowered his arm, placed the water balloon in the trash can, and muttered "thanks" as he walked away. Despite challenging conditions, the Oasis management mission requires provision of consistent limits without negative labels. No matter what, staff members almost always seem to provide a safe and positive environment—the kind that most of these adolescents have never before experienced.

Daily Challenges

In addition to running interference with residents, counselors must constantly respond to the incoming crisis calls and outgoing negotiations with officials from Juvenile Justice, the Department of Human Services, agencies providing clothing and other supplies, parents, and family members. During one of our interviews, a staff member interrupted our discussions to take a crisis call from an adolescent. He quickly and effectively determined the youth's emotional status and immediate needs. He then called an apartment complex, a local thrift store, the young person's mother, and made a return call to the youth to report progress in his on-the-fly case management. These four rapid-fire calls are typical of a Counselor-on-Duty's (COD's) shift responsibilities.

Being temporary facilities, the building was understandably not ideally suited to the shelter program. The building was a somewhat rambling, one-story structure in which the sleeping rooms were down the hall from the front office, creating substantial supervision problems. Moreover, the facility resided on a campus of buildings in which there were other residential programs unrelated to Oasis. While staff protocol called for regular room checks throughout the night, the physical plant seemed to invite peeping toms from other programs, uninvited guests to adolescent residents through bedroom windows, and sneaking out on the part of residents themselves. These dynamics added another layer of stress and challenges to a staff that was already coping with a situation that (at times) seemed impossible.

Accommodations at The Village physically distanced shelter staff from the rest of the agency. Another worrisome feature of the arrangement was that a 20-minute drive to the main agency building created a hardship on staff members who needed to attend meetings and other activities while simultaneously being responsible for providing constant supervision and support for residents.

The day-in, day-out stress from being surrogate parents to surly adolescents, from working in a crowded and dilapidated environment, and from the isolation and estrangement of the rest of the agency should have added up to negativity, cynicism, and burnout. Despite the abysmal setting created by the tragedy of fire, however, came an enthusiasm and exuberant commitment to the program from virtually everyone on the shelter team. Repeatedly, we heard and observed an almost reverent dedication to the core mission of Oasis and a genuine love of the opportunities found there for personal and professional growth. When asked about Oasis' greatest strength, Frances Rich, bearer of the condom containing trashcan, emphasized, "Our commitment to teens. . . no one else believes in them like we do." Frances' sentiments were echoed by program director Sherry Allen, who told us that the role of the shelter is to "help young people make informed choices." She has mountains of evidence showing that the shelter program has consistently been able to meet that goal. On the occasion of one resident's birthday, a staff member bought a cake at her own expense when no family members showed up to care. On another occasion, a resident who fled an abusive home was taken to a second-hand store to select appropriate clothing. George Mensah, a native of Liberia with an infectious smile, revealed his sheer enjoyment of the challenge of being in the midst of shelter activity. While Mensah was able to articulate some agency weaknesses when pressed, he concluded, "The work is of such value that the weaknesses seem petty."

TURNING AROUND ADVERSITY

What is the magical potion or rare ingredient that can create staff enthusiasm and commitment from such environmental adversity and overwhelming work demands? Our research revealed three dynamics that were primarily responsible for making it all possible: 1) leadership that listens—the creation of a highly participatory management environment; 2) creativity and flexibility; and 3) caring and respect (both personally and professionally).

Leadership That Listens

Every shelter employee whom we interviewed felt that an important element in the strong shelter program was the fact that Program Director Sherry Allen listened. "Sherry gets a lot out of people because she sees good in people and expects that to come out," one associate said. "Sherry can communicate needed changes in non-punitive ways."

Sherry's leadership style was described as "nurturing" and "a most maternal administration." While our first round of observations suggested that this technique might be simply characteristic of her individual style, we later came to understand that most staff members knew that style was deliberately chosen. Sherry intends for her actions to communicate and educate—and most of the time, she achieves these goals. In staff meetings, for example, time is always devoted to relationships among staff, conflict resolution, and consensus building in decision making. That sends a strong message that these things are important. These techniques and messages are then passed through to clients, who have had precious little exposure to these critical interpersonal skills. For example, when a concern is raised among staff, Sherry takes time to solicit opinions from everyone who is present. She then integrates opinions into a summary statement and asks whether her summary accurately reflects the opinions offered. Similarly, staff demonstrate this active listening with residents who all too often have not had adults care about their opinions. Sherry will sort offered problem solutions against agency policy, highlighting those that are consistent with the guidelines. In the same vein, staff will work to incorporate resident suggestions as long as they are consistent with shelter policies. Again, youth can be heard, but within appropriate boundaries. Again and again, you will hear staff members talk about treating clients as they have been treated as employees.

A Need for Collegiality

As researchers, we began to see the shelter staff as a metaphor of "the good little wife" syndrome—that stigmatized image of the good mother who stays home away from contacts with other adult peers because child-care duties are so demanding that no time is available for other important things such as education and personal development. One problem that our qualitative research revealed was the status differential that had existed within the shelter staff. Residential staff who provide 24-hour coverage and who supervise residents in their daily routines are largely bachelor degree-level employees, while the counselors who work daily in more formal individual and family therapy tend to have masters degrees and some type of license. As tension surfaced around this perceived (and, according to our data, real) differential, considerable staff meeting time was spent establishing the effectiveness levels of *all* staff members. For example, they identified important ways in which every contact with an adolescent was therapeutic, not just the formal time spent with the counseling staff. Soon, the assignment board in the office changed, and where there had been an assigned counselor for each resident, there came to be an assigned team of counselor/residential staff members who conferred regularly to develop the youth's daily therapeutic plan. Staff meetings were instituted for the night shift, and Sherry Allen attended—despite the fact that they occurred at 11 P.M., after an already full day. From start to finish, this in-house intervention was based on skillful listening.

Skillful listening involves the full utilization of the staff team. These solutions were not Sherry's creation. Rather, they came from team members who felt safe expressing both their frustrations and proposed solutions in a non-judgmental setting. Clarification of the different roles of both residential and clinical staff occurred, and more importantly, how these roles could complement one another (rather than colliding into tension and competition). In her recent book about person-centered leadership (Plas, 1996), one of our authors underscores that "successful teams—no matter where you find them—are made up of individuals who know how to define roles for themselves and how to work with the roles that other team members have adopted" (p. 86). Residential staff could articulate their important role with youth, and formal counselors gained a new appreciation of their role while reciprocally helping residential staff understand their roles more fully.

It is no coincidence that in the front of the Oasis *Counselor on Duty* manual, right after the introduction and security information, you will find four pages of detailed notes titled, "Listening Techniques." The art of listening, according to the manual, requires availability, concentration, active participation, and comprehension. Listening entails not only attention to words but also to feelings and implied symbolic meanings. "Listening is a skill—a skill that must be learned, developed, and practiced to be useful," according to the manual. This statement is written, of course, in the context of staff listening to clients. The value is demonstrated day in and day out, however, as leadership listens to staff and colleagues listen to one another. Each person intentionally encourages by example.

Down-Side Characteristics

This type of participatory management has certain down-side characteristics that an agency interested in implementing this strategy should consider. The first is shared by virtually all participatory-management structures: the time commitment required to genuinely solicit staff opinions and involvement. "We meet to death," "Our model is not time efficient," and "It takes forever to make a decision" are typical comments from our shelter interviews. An autocratic, top-down decision might be efficient, but it loses valuable payoffs in terms of employee involvement, the creation of feelings of worth and personal commitment, and the high-quality ideas that emerge when people feel encouraged to be creative. While shelter staff members voice the time-consuming reality of participatory management, they would have it no other way.

Another dominant concern that participatory-management organizations in the United States often experience is uneven team development and less-than-adequate cross-team fertilization. Like the United States, many western countries have developed deep commitments to departmentalized functioning. Typically, it is hard for participatory-management organizations to move quickly toward a model of easy communication across teams. At Oasis, we observed that active listening and participatory management was alive and well within the shelter team and within other agency teams, but it was weak across teams. Shelter staff perceived central-office staff as aloof, non-involved, or uncaring. Shelter people seemed to have a sense of being in the trenches together as a team, but without a clear line of communication from command central. This phenomenon perhaps made them closer as a team, but at the sacrifice of overall agency loyalty. Many factors that were unique to the Oasis situation might have contributed: the fire and the difficulties of shelter staff being housed temporarily in the main agency building;

the distance of the temporary shelter from other agency activities; or agency leadership not demonstrating the same level of commitment to participatory management that the shelter leadership displayed. One staff members voiced the frustration that the shelter program was the showpiece of the fundraising efforts, yet this person felt left out of development strategies by the larger agency organization. When interns were selected and assigned to agency programs, the shelter intern slots were typically the last to be filled.

Organizational loyalty at a smaller unit of analysis (for example, the individual team) does not necessarily preclude organizational loyalty at a more global level. These issues need careful consideration, however. Is participatory management being implemented locally or universally throughout an organization? Who buys into the principles and concepts of participatory management and active listening? Is this management style embraced sporadically or universally? How does a fledgling participatory-management organization successfully defeat old, culturally ingrained tendencies toward departmentalization and territoriality? These important questions must be considered.

Creativity and Flexibility

We spoke earlier of the staff manual, an important tool in the agency's arsenal of resources. Make no mistake, however—while there is an excellent and detailed staff manual, this agency is by no means a "by the book" organization. Repeatedly, the manual highlights the roles of creativity and flexibility. The passage in the manual that says, "This is your shift; what are you going to do?" communicates that individual staff members are to be creative and spontaneous with clients. Sherry Allen told us that one of her goals is to encourage staff to ask, "Why not?" Her colleagues are constantly evaluating their daily activities to determine what works and what does not.

Warren Bennis (1989) suggested that transformative leaders should "create visions of potential opportunities for organizations, instill within employees commitment to change. . . and build confidence and empower their employees to seek new ways of doing things" (p. 18). He describes great leadership not so much as the use of power but as the empowerment of others and the capacity to build self-esteem. Michelle Hall's experience is a reflection of this principle. Hall first came to the shelter program as a social-work intern. "This population intimidated me," she says. "I was truly challenged by the kids. I had to overcome my natural shyness. But I learned that I do my best work when I'm uncomfortable. The staff made me feel comfortable enough to try my own style and try different things. I now know that I'm good at connecting with kids on a personal level. That I care. Oasis does that—it allows individuals to use their individual strengths to be creative with clients." Despite her initial inexperience, Michelle was allowed to find her own rhythm and style in working with the adolescents, and it paid off in personal and professional growth for her as well as for Oasis, which gained a future permanent staffer.

Frances Rich echoed Michelle's sentiments. "I was raised with limitations, and at Oasis I realized that limitations do not exist," she says. "I've developed supervisory skills and presentation skills and been encouraged to get licensure and certification. I've received lots of positive feedback." Frances also spoke about her own style and the opportunities to grow both personally and professionally. She reflected on the importance of constantly evaluating daily activities and making changes that enhance staff effectiveness with teens. This orientation might seem reminiscent of the old corporate quality-control circles begun in Japan by Dr. Kaoru Ishikawa (Ross, 1982). The fundamental goals of those activities were (a) to contribute to the improvement and development of the enterprise; (b) to respect humanity and to build worthwhile lives and cheerful workplaces; and (c) to give fullest rein to human capabilities and to draw out each individual's infinite potential (Ishikawa, 1985). While all three of these goals are important at Oasis, their model is arguably richer than a quality-circles approach—because this organization is committed to person-centered management and the continual development of staff members' personal and professional potentials.

The creative development of individuals produces amazing side effects. Take Frances Rich's case. In addition to the dreary accommodations inside the temporary shelter building, Oasis was allocated an inadequate total of three parking spaces outside. Staff and visitors therefore had to park on a grassy area immediately in front of the building. When it rained, however, the grassy area became a mud-filled nightmare, making getting from the car to the building difficult. Miraculously, gravel one day appeared on the parking muck. All of a sudden, the area had become a pleasant and safe area. Eventually, people discovered that once again, a staff member made no distinction between personal and professional needs. Frances had donated time to bring her own tractor over the weekend to spread the gravel. This kind of staff commitment pays off.

Respect and Caring

Inherent in the values of empowerment and creative flexibility is a core principle of respect and caring for the employee. "The employee is as important as the people we serve," says Frances Rich. "We play well together, on the job and after hours. In prior jobs, I was afraid to laugh. Here, it is encouraged and is a part of staff meetings." Rich's sentiments are mirrored by other staff. George Mensah highlighted the importance of taking care of oneself and having fun. Our own experience is consonant with George's emphasis. Having served as a facilitator for countless staff retreats and planning sessions at other for-profit and nonprofit organizations, we have concluded that the normative agenda in this country has emphasized filling those times with a work-related focus and task orientation. Our participation in an Oasis shelter program retreat reflected a newer, more person-centered approach. The first half of the day was spent in team-building exercises and planning for shelter initiatives. In marked contrast to other retreats, the afternoon was spent on a paddlewheel boat enjoying the Nashville skyline and one another's company.

Sherry Allen highlights that the respect is not just top down but also bottom up. "At Oasis, it's okay to screw up, to have fun, to laugh, and to cry," she says. "This is a place to be human. I can come in to work and say, 'I'm going to be bitchy today; let me know if I get out of hand.'" Sherry knows that sentiment is respected and that people will simply do as she asks, giving her feedback if her disposition becomes troublesome.

Another strength of the Oasis sense of respect and caring comes from the comfortable position that at Oasis, being a parent is easy. While Sherry is willing to attend night-shift staff meetings, she also appreciates the understanding provided by staff when her own children need attention. When she has to handle child-care demands, others cover her responsibilities at Oasis without hesitation and with enthusiasm. A spirit of mutuality pervades the shelter staff team. They support one another on a personal and professional level.

CONTINUING IMPROVEMENT

The Oasis shelter staff provides an excellent example of adversity turned to strength and optimism. The staff reflects a service-agency program that continues to creatively serve clients and adapt programming to fit less-than-ideal working .conditions. At the new shelter's open house, Sherry Allen spoke of the strength in the staff brainstorming after the fire. "We have come to a deeper understanding of homelessness, of being in transition, of anxiety about an unknown future—all issues that the youth we serve feel constantly," she said. The music by Native Americans and the children's games were symbols of the inclusiveness that is an important part of the Oasis culture. The cheery decor and coordinated color schemes donated by the local chapter of interior designers will surely soothe the frayed nerves of teens who are seeking refuge as they also promote healing and understanding.

Our initial research phase concluded about the time of the new shelter dedication. Yet, it remained an open question whether or not the shelter team could shed its stepchild position.

The Phase Two inquiry indicated that a good program was becoming an even better one. In a follow-up phone interview, Sherry Allen noted increased staff morale and confidence. The new facility, whose planning included heavy input from the shelter staff themselves, lends itself to staff providing adequate resident supervision while also providing space for teens to be alone when needed. Sherry wryly lamented the lack of constant crisis in the old transitional building, such as teens climbing out of windows in the middle of the night. "But, we have new problems now—just this week, half of our youth requested extensions of their [standard two week] stay at the shelter," she says. Bricks and mortar often become symbolic of visions and dreams. When the original shelter burned, the Capital Campaign shifted emphasis from the agency building to the new shelter that was needed. The successful completion of both the fundraising and the building project helped to erase the previous stepchild image of the shelter program. The crisis call line is now housed in the shelter, and there has been an increase of 250 percent in crisis calls and walk-ins. Sherry Allen calls the shelter "the coolest spot we've got." More all-agency meetings are now held at the shelter.

The building is not the only element that has strengthened the shelter program. As with other Oasis programs, the Shelter Team has actively worked to build upon an already-firm program base. Shelter counselors now devote time each week to street outreach. They go into the Nashville community looking for homeless youth (at the bus depot, at the downtown homeless service center, and even under bridges). Much of this work is done in the afternoons and evenings, when youth are not concerned about being picked up for truancy. In 1998–1999, Oasis reach 645 youth through this program.

Now, at the conclusion of our study, Frances Rich (former shelter counselor) serves as shelter director. When we first met Frances, she felt challenged in fresh, new ways that she had not experienced in previous employment settings. She was learning to laugh and to have fun. Frances used her natural gifts in creative but effective ways. "This is just what I want to do," she stated at the time. So now, as shelter director, does she miss doing what she just want[ed] to do? "Why, no, it's Oasis!" she says. Once again, Frances expresses amazement at her new level of self-confidence. "I never dreamed of being a director," she says. Frances now applies her people skills—formerly used so effectively with residents—with the staff associates whom she supervises. Sure, Frances has the daily administrative hassles of dealing with occasional property damage or a malfunctioning alarm system. But she understands and applies the core Oasis principles learned so well: respecting the organizational culture, nurturing and empowering the individual both personally and professionally, giving them room for creative growth, confronting constructively, and developing strong teams.

Leadership that listens, fostering creativity and flexibility, and respect and caring that trickles downward and percolates upward are all of the ingredients that the Oasis shelter staff uses to serve troubled teens who have no other place to go. First, however, they decided that they had to use them in conjunction with each other.

Strategies for Practice

In a person-centered environment, strategies of customer care must first be applied to staff associates. Successful leadership includes the following components:

- Consistent and respectful listening

- Support for risk-taking, creativity, and flexibility

- Caring and respect for the individual, both personally and professionally

The art of listening requires the following:

- *Availability*—When possible, have an open-door policy where associates feel comfortable just dropping by to talk. Enlist the support of your administrative assistant in this endeavor. Also, get out of the office every day and visit with staff in their work spaces. Over time, make certain that you talk with every employee, including the custodian.

- *Concentration*—Maintain eye contact. Work at the skills of listening exclusively, rather than thinking ahead to formulate a response while the other is still speaking. Stop other activities that could be distracting.

- *Active participation*—Suspend your own judgment and invite more information with statements such as, "I'd like to hear more about what you are saying," or "Is there anything more you want me to know?" Ask open questions.

- *Comprehension*—Summarize what you have heard in order to ensure accuracy. For example, begin by saying, "I'd like to run back what you've just told me to be sure I've got it." Avoid *why* questions, because they can be challenging and blaming and can call upon the other person to justify or defend something.

- *Attention to words, feelings, and symbolic meanings*—Pay attention to body language and non-verbal cues that indicate mood. Again, check out feelings of the other person with a statement such as, "You sound as if this situation makes you really angry."

Listening skills are learned skills. Look for a workshop or seminar, or bring in a consultant who can help you and your leadership learn active listening. Also, in a person-centered environment, learning these skills will reap benefits not only in the work place, but also in your personal development.

- Support for risk-taking, creativity, and flexibility is a hallmark of person-centered management. Part of your "walking around" listening can include specific questions regarding innovative ideas of associates and encouragement for them to pursue these ideas. Important in this process, then, are follow-up inquiries as to how the new idea or project is taking hold. True interest and support is not a one-shot deal. Be specific in acknowledging creative efforts of associates, and be clear that there is no condemnation for appropriate experimentation. "What a great idea whose time has not yet come!" might be appropriate for a risk-taking idea that did not work.

- Caring and respect for the individual, both personally and professionally, is inherent in this model. "How can I help you be more effective in your work?" Pay attention to personal concerns, as well, while maintaining a respectful distance and not prying too closely. Again, follow up. For example, if a staff associate experiences a family death, you would certainly acknowledge that loss at the time with a personal word and appropriate gesture. A truly person-centered manager will make a point to ask again how things are going two weeks or two months later.
  Caution: Challenges to participatory management include exceptional time commitment and a tendency to polarize within teams.

REFERENCES

Bennis, W. (1989). *On becoming a leader*. Reading, MA: Addison-Wesley.

Ishikawa, K. (1985). *What is total quality control? The Japanese way*. Englewood Cliffs, NJ: Prentice Hall.

Plas, Jeanne M. (1996). *Person-centered leadership: An American approach to participatory management*. Thousand Oaks, CA: Sage Publications, Inc.

Ross, P. (1982). *The future of Canada's auto industry: The big three and the Japanese challenge*. Toronto: Canadian Institute for Economic Policy.

9

A Vital and Vibrant Infrastructure
Teamwork That Works

Historically, the Oasis Center has used a traditional management flow-chart—that tree of boxes cascading down the page from the board of directors that reflects the chain of command, supervisory responsibilities, and proper pecking order. At Oasis, this flowchart did not reflect reality. Once again, the culture tells the real story. The heart and soul of Oasis management lies within its program teams. While *team* is the contemporary buzz word as well as a successful management tool, particularly in corporate America, the Oasis teams could almost be considered organizational families—although we will continue to refer to them as teams in this chapter.

Figure 9-1 depicts our interpretation of the Oasis management flowchart. At center stage are the various program teams that work closely with each other in order to support growth and development in clients and their families. The program teams have inter-member support and connectedness, and while there is some hierarchy within any given team, responsibility and decision-making resides within the whole team. Liz Allen Fey, associate executive director, sums up the situation this way: "Oasis is a learning organization with shared ownership. We work better in groups than alone."

The Oasis philosophy suggests that the Management Team—which consists of central administrative personnel and Program Team leaders—provides a servant-leadership role, committing resources to supply the needs of the various ongoing programs. Similarly, the board of directors channels its

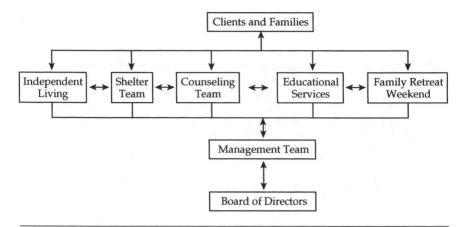

Figure 9.1. Oasis Management Flowchart (author's interpretation)

energies to support Oasis programs and leadership with fiscal and community resources to assist successful program implementation for clients and their families. This system is bottom-up, rather than top-down. In this vein, Warren Bennis (1989) describes leadership not so much as the use of power but of the empowerment of others—the capacity to build self-esteem in workers. Plas' (1996) person-centered leadership expands this idea to give as much attention to personal and professional development of staff as to clients and services.

TEAM LEADERS

In this spirit, team leaders project themselves and act largely in the role of peer team member and coach, rather than team leader. Yet, they do provide leadership in advocating for resources from the larger organization and providing guidance (but not necessarily solutions) when problems arise. For example, Receptionist Angela Hines describes her Support-Services supervisor, Deanna Scales, as "firm, but flexible. . . not too serious." Betty Everett, Educational Services team leader, receives kudos from her team members. "Her management style is great; similar to teaching," says Paige McClain. "I am my own boss with excellent supervision." Another associate describes Everett's feedback as "great" and describes her as an "exhorter," which Webster defines as one who incites and encourages. Jill Baker, leader of the

Independent Living team, is an unusual hire from outside the agency when several current employees had applied for the position. Charlotte Mann, overnight relief worker in Independent Living, says that "Jill came in and made others feel part of the team." As a part-time overnight worker, Charlotte is always invited and included in team meetings. Irma Ecksel, another Independent Living team member, concurs: "What seems like little supervision is a way of caretaking. . . it gives me room to grow." Examples of other team leaders are consistently positive.

The team philosophy starts at the beginning. All hiring interviews are team based. Eric Fogle, who has been with Oasis for two years, still recalls his initial team interview vividly. "Denise, Judy, Liz, and Rebekah were all there," he says. "It was a different model." Irma Ecksel viewed the group interview as an inquisition and later found that interviewers thought the session was relaxed. Former intern Lewis went through a team interview but did not find it intimidating. Team interviewing is consistent with servant leadership and the Oasis philosophy. No team leader at Oasis would ever make a hiring decision solo.

Group Versus Team

Before exploring the critical elements of teams, we want to note the differences between groups and teams (Douglass & Douglass, 1992), because many people think that a group and a team are the same. Teamwork is far more demanding and far more rewarding than group work. Groups are organizational entities pulled together for primarily administrative purposes. In a group, communication is more controlled, and conformity is often more important than results. Rather than participating in the decision-making process, group members are often told what to do, and members work more independently than dependently. We highlight this distinction because Oasis, which is so team oriented, seems to try to make its groups into teams. One example is its staff meetings.

As an intern at Oasis during part of the initial research, Lewis attended numerous team meetings of the shelter staff as well as general agency-wide gatherings. Both forums demonstrate the key elements of group and individual attention, but the striking difference between the two is the depth and intensity levels at which these key elements are played out. The comparisons and contrasts in tone, enthusiasm, and perceived level of commitment are striking. Both settings provide opportunities for kudos and personal sharing. At some level, both welcome input, new ideas, and alternative opinions. For example, in a year where no salary increases were budgeted, a plan was devised for quarterly bonuses (should a surplus exist for that quarter). When someone in the general staff meeting pointed out that an across-the-board percentage bonus was regressive, giving higher-salaried employees larger bonuses, the executive director indicated a willingness to review the policy. Later in the Shelter Team meeting, however, much more honest expressions about work and compensation parity surfaced.

Similarly, in both settings, a surprisingly high level of willingness exists to volunteer for that extra presentation outside the organization or that extra set of hands in order to meet a deadline. That is the Oasis way. When gravel was donated to ease the mud situation in a temporary shelter parking lot, a counselor brought her personal tractor over on a Saturday to spread the gravel. Rarely an agency-wide meeting goes by without a request for someone to speak to this civic group or that school. Ready volunteers are always available.

While there are similar elements in both Program Team meetings and staff meetings, the former are clearly teams and the latter are groups. Oasis seems to not acknowledge and accept this distinction and frets, in its self-critical way, about how to make staff meetings more team-like (although Oasis might not use those words). Oasis has staff meetings to discuss how to improve staff meetings. Employees experiment with different formats, leadership, and agenda styles. While this situation is fine, Oasis, with teamwork as a core value, seems to want to create true teamwork in every meeting. Recognizing where teams are effective in your organization and where they are not is essential.

EFFECTIVE TEAMS: THE CRITICAL ELEMENTS

Plas (1996) notes that all too often, businesses rush to develop teams within their organizations, hand out tasks and assignments, and then wonder in amazement when the team does not function well or produce optimal results. Our western (and more specifically, American) culture trains us to think and work as individualists. When we come together as members of a team, we all too often still think individually and hierarchically, looking for an identified leader of the group who will give guidance and direction and explain our roles and tasks. "Real teamwork is about shared responsibility and action, as well as shared decision making. Difference of position does not mean inequality of position" (Plas, p. 78). As discussed in Chapter 2, however, for teams to be successful in our American culture, the individual cannot be lost. Equal attention must be given to individual development and recognition as is provided for team development and recognition. Therefore, it is not surprising that critical elements of teamwork include individual encouragement and support, as well. Routhieaux and Higgins (1999) say, "Our research suggests that ignoring the concerns and well-being of individual team members, through lack of rewards, recognition, or support, limits the potential benefits of teamwork regardless of how successful the team is in accomplishing its objectives" (p. 29). We introduced these ideas in Chapter 4, but we wish to focus on them now as they specifically apply to Oasis.

Goal Clarity

Teams must stay in touch with how their work specifically supports the larger organizational goals. Sherry Allen frequently reminds shelter staff that the purpose is to "help young people make informed choices." As staff associates report on client cases, they explicitly cite examples as to how this process works. Weekend Family Retreat Associate Cheryl Neville acknowledges that the Weekend Family Retreat program "reaches families in a unique way."

Individual and Collective Growth

As we discussed, individuals are encouraged to push themselves and to grow personally and professionally. These individual efforts have a direct impact on teamwork. Irma Ecksel, educational specialist for the Independent Living team, feels that she has found her niche at Oasis and is "amazed at how much I like it here and how good I am at it." Her positive growth spills over to the Independent Living team and subsequently to the clients. Irma describes a middle-class white girl who chose to date African-American men. Her family threw her out, and she came to the Oasis Independent Living program. This young woman graduated from high school and received a scholarship for college. She subsequently went to graduate school, working two jobs and buying a car. Irma is quick to emphasize that this young woman's success was a team effort.

Similarly, a now 22-year-old once painted her room black and destroyed the girls' bathroom at her high school with graffiti. At age 18, this young woman was on suicide watch. She recently visited Oasis and exclaimed, "Boy, if I knew then what I know now. You ought to have me back there as a speaker!" Again, individual growth impinges upon staff team growth in a positive outcome for a client.

Flexibility

Oasis associates are encouraged to use their individual strengths to be creative with clients. Individual creativity and flexibility spill over to teamwork. Creative brainstorming is commonplace in team meetings, with ideas displayed on charts around the room. Outlandish ideas are respected and considered. Eric Fogle describes the Oasis flexibility as "unbelievably rampant." Eric states that disagreements are viewed as just another way to approach a problem or challenge.

Trusting Relationships

Trust is built over time through personal interactions that are rewarding, honest, and accepting. Oasis associates work at trust-building through these kinds of interactions. Michelle Hall notes that time is consistently allocated in meetings for relationship-building and personal sharing. Michelle adds, "We need that [trust] when we're dealing with a crisis. The style is passed along to clients." Program teams structure team retreats to expressly focus on trust development through team-building exercises.

Willingness to Confront

We believe that this element of effective teams is one of the Oasis challenges. Perhaps the values of growth and trust are in juxtaposition with confrontation, and managers and staff are reticent to confront an effort to foster teamwork.

Team Mistakes

When there are difficulties in team performance or relationships, those are acknowledged in a non-punitive way and are dealt with creatively.

An incident occurred one night at the shelter in which non-residents were allowed into resident bedrooms through the windows. One might surmise that night-shift personnel were not following supervision protocol precisely. Yet, in the team meeting, no finger pointing occurred, and plans for shoring up security were developed thoughtfully and creatively.

In the area of team relationships, the Oasis openness to self-critique and growth stems from the core of the Management Team itself. The executive director, business administrator, and associate director were struggling with interpersonal and professional issues and how their differences might affect the agency and its future. Rather than attempting to minimize these difficulties to us as researchers, these agency leaders invited us to participate in several sessions with them and provide direct intervention designed to clarify and facilitate a better understanding of their roles and relationships. Management Team meetings provide time for personal check-ins. The Management Team was broadened to include program directors, specialists, and the volunteer coordinator. Team members rotate chairing the meetings. This team, as others, is not afraid to admit difficulties and address them.

WITHIN VERSUS BETWEEN

During our initial investigation, we found the within-team strengths strikingly abundant. Peggy Christian's comment, "I can't imagine not having feedback from my team" and another person's comment, "There's a total lack of power struggles within teams" are typical of sentiments expressed. We also found that the between-team relationships were often weak, frayed, or non-existent, however. Comments range from innocuous, such as "There's not much interaction across teams" to stronger words describing the across-team relationships, such as "splintering" and "petty." Several associates complained that "some teams were valued more than others." Program Team members and their leaders were concerned about the level of support of the Management Team. For example, the Weekend Family Retreat team gave a two-hour in-service workshop, and no one from the Management Team attended. Even worse, internal friction existed among some members of the Management Team. Board of director members did not personally know many staff workers and did not have a full understanding of the daily workings of the organization. These deficiencies made board members less articulate advocates for Oasis in fundraising and community support.

This situation raises an either-or question. To achieve the incredible level of within-team coordination and cooperation, must between-team communication necessarily suffer? Is it possible to have both levels working harmoniously and not have to choose one or the other? Put another way, an important dilemma in team development and functioning is the balance between differentiation, or specialization, of a team or small work group and integration of the team members into the larger organization (Beer & Walton, 1987; Burke, 1993). Analogous to a figure-ground problem in perception, must emphasis on small-group cohesiveness (for example, teams) weaken the overall organizational culture? In the spirit of Oasis philosophy (discussed in Chapter 4), the management *and* staff took this question seriously and worked creatively in order to resolve the difficulties.

Yet, a much deeper level of honesty and commitment exists at the Program Team level. Again, to speak of the program teams as an organizational family, there is a deeper level of intimacy. Problem solving is never about finding fault. Opinions are not only respected but are actively solicited. Alternatives are generated before solutions are determined. This level of intimacy seems consistent within each of the Program Teams and not unique to any one team. Members of the Counseling Team spoke of utilizing various client approaches on themselves in the team meetings. Staff would share their own family foibles through genograms (diagrams of family structure and dynamics) just as they would plot trans-generational trends with their clients. Creativity and risk-taking is infused throughout the Oasis culture and manifests itself particularly within the Program Teams.

The richer depth of intimacy within Program Teams might be explained, in part, not only by the deeper level of trust in those Program Team meetings but also by the geographical proximity of program staff and relative isolation from other program personnel. Staff from the Shelter and Independent Living programs, in particular, were housed in separate buildings several miles from the main office building, and the Educational Services team was divided into two locations. Even in the main agency building, staff members of the Counseling Team and the Weekend Family Retreat were on separate floors. Logically, therefore, daily casual contact was much more frequent within Program Teams than between the other teams.

ORGANIZATIONAL WEAKNESSES: MAKING IT BETTER

We go back to the either-or question, "Does the closeness within the Program Teams preclude similar feelings and processes in the larger organization?" Must there intrinsically be a we-they tension? Oasis staff, at least, are not willing to say yes. Cross-team collaborations are formed around agency-wide issues that brought staff together with diverse orientations, perceptions, and priorities. Debra Grimes writes:

> When an issue is brought to the management's attention that is blocking staff from performing at their best, information is solicited from all program teams

as well as suggestions for resolution. If a resolution is clear, implementation is assigned to the most appropriate program or individual and then communicated back to the staff members. If a resolution is not clear a cross-program team is gathered to work on a solution. One of the most effective teams is the cultural diversity team which has challenged all the staff members to examine their beliefs and created a very accepting environment.

The salary issue is another example. Rather than leaving that dilemma to the Management Team, staff from all levels of the agency worked together to formulate an equitable salary structure. The format and location of the general staff meetings underwent experimentation and revision. Opportunities were consciously created to facilitate staff from different Program Teams to interact informally and develop more solid trust levels. Eric Fogle described an Adoption Program in which associates adopt one another to consciously take time to connect both personally and professionally. Eric adopted the executive director and was adopted himself by Paige McClain. Programmatically, associates from the Counseling Team now lead multi-family groups in the shelter.

Despite these positive efforts that did improve cross-team connections to some extent, our follow-up research confirmed that primary team involvement continued to take priority. Sherry Allen, previous shelter director and recent associate executive director, concurred that associates by and large "love their own team." She underscored, however, that this team loyalty did not detract from work across teams or from feelings of loyalty for the overall agency. In essence, "they do not compete," she says. Sherry noted that while Oasis strives to be as flat an agency as possible, cross-team comfort is somewhat a degree of position. It is understandable that program directors communicate across teams more readily than front-line staff. In fact, program directors now meet regularly, separate from the Management Team, to share ideas and to seek fresh perspective from peers on any issues.

SENSE OF COMMUNITY

As researchers, we pondered the feedback that we received regarding commitment to work teams. During our investigation, we had formed the impression from qualitative interviews that belief in, and commitment to, the overall agency of Oasis was exceptional. With the repeated comments regarding strength of teams, we decided to check our original hypothesis with a small quantitative questionnaire conducted by phone regarding feelings toward the overall agency. We used the four dimensions consistently cited in the community psychology literature as components of sense of community: 1) membership, a sense of belonging, identification, and personal investment; 2) influence; 3) getting needs met; and 4) an emotional connection (McMillan & Chavis, 1986). We also added a fifth dimension of loyalty, which we had found relevant in a previous sense of community study (Plas & Lewis, 1996). We asked associates to rate these components on a scale of one to 10, with one being "not at all" and 10 being "extremely so." We specifically asked associates to respond in the context of their individual relationship with the overall agency. Our sample was not large enough for statistical significance, but the results were nonetheless supportive in a positive direction that a strong sense of community exists among associates for Oasis as a whole. The strongest endorsements were for a feeling of membership (9) and a sense of loyalty (9.33). Other average ratings included influence (8.67), needs met (6.67), and emotional connection (8).

Finally, we asked associates for a summary score (using all five dimensions) of their sense of community for both the overall agency and their individual teams. Both were high, although sense of community for the individual team (9.33) was slightly stronger than that of the overall agency (8).

One of our original questions had addressed whether team development and strength necessarily detracted from positive feelings toward the agency as a whole. Despite the small sample, these data give us no indication that this situation is the case (at least, at Oasis). Associates express a high level of commitment and belief in the mission of the agency and give manifestation to that commitment through their daily work in their respective program team.

At Oasis, teamwork works. Associates are aware of the critical elements of successful teams and exercise them continually through a delicate balance of attention to the individual *and* to the group.

Strategies for Practice: Teamwork

- Develop teams around function—Each team must develop its own mission statement and articulate how the team mission statement fits with the organizational mission statement. Revisit this fit on a periodic basis.

- Individual ideas must be heard, respected, and considered—Make sure that the individual is not lost in the team effort.

- Make a distinction between process and production of the team—Production has to do with who will do what in order to accomplish the group's goal. Process deals with how the team will get up and function smoothly as a unit.

- Team leaders function as coaches, rather than directors—They delegate decision-making to the team.

True teams demonstrate the following characteristics:

- Goal clarity

- Individual and collective growth

- Flexibility

- Trusting relationships

- Willingness to confront

- Acceptance of team mistakes

- Strong team members tend to focus energy more on intra-team work, rather than on cross-team collaboration (although not exclusively).

- Positive teamwork fosters a sense of community in the workplace.

REFERENCES

Beer, M. and Walton, A. E. (1987). Organization change and development. *Annual Review of Psychology*, Volume 38, pp. 339–367.

Bennis, W. (1989). *On becoming a leader*. Reading, MA: Addison-Wesley.

Burke, W. (1993). *Organization development* (2nd ed.). Reading, MA: Addison-Wesley.

Douglass, M. E. and Douglass, D. N. (1992). *Time management for teams*. New York: American Management Association.

McMillan, D. W. and Chavis, D. M. (1986). Sense of community: A definition and theory. *Journal of Community Psychology*, Volume 14, pp. 6–23.

Plas, J. M. (1996). *Person-centered leadership: An American approach to participatory management*. Thousand Oaks, CA: Sage Publications, Inc.

Routhieaux, R. L. and Higgins, S. E. (1999). The effective team member: Avoiding team burnout. *The Health Care Manager*, Volume 18, pp. 29–34.

Plas, J. M. and Lewis, S. E. (1996). Environmental factors and sense of community in a planned town. *American Journal of Community Psychology*, Volume 24, pp. 109–143.

10

The Future of Nonprofit Participatory Management

As so many (Block, 1987; Deal & Kennedy, 1999; & Mann, 1989) have pointed out, participatory management is here to stay. In fact, participatory management is likely to continue to be the most highly touted management strategy and one of the most heavily relied-upon models of the 21st century. Little question exists, however, that organizations of all sorts have reported a wide range of results on a success-failure continuum. Some participatory models have worked well in certain settings and have stood the test of time. Many more have failed (c.f., Pitt, 1994; Reina & Reina, 1999; & Schrage, 1995).

THE POSSIBILITIES

The core of all participatory-management models is empowerment (Blanchard, Carlos, & Randolph, 1999; Bracey, Rosenblum, Sanford, & Trueblood, 1990; & Whitney, 1994). Philosophically, workers who are staffing the unit's front line are believed to grasp the issues and problems in an especially fundamental way. The leadership empowers associates to make the decisions that are within their areas of responsibility and expertise. Employees make the decisions that count.

As Argyris (1998) noted, "Considering its much touted potential, it's no wonder that empowerment receives all the attention it does" (p. 98).

Theoretically, these models empower senior leaders to develop employees at all levels of the company. Associates are encouraged to take informed risks and to use creative skills on behalf of the organization's mission. Indeed, all employees are encouraged to co-create mission statements that actually guide action within their units. Individuals are motivated to think of themselves as associates who labor within a learning environment, where the acquisition of knowledge and skills is expected to be a lifelong pursuit that the organization supports. Employees become committed. More committed employees produce better products, services, and a host of dynamics that create excellent organizations. While the theory is so logical and so appealing, however, the realities too often fall far short. What is the problem?

THE REALITIES

In an especially cogent analysis of the problem, Argyris (1998) explains the difficulties in terms of the issue of commitment. He points out that we have learned that individuals develop internal commitment to the organization and their roles within it when *they* define the tasks, the behavior required to execute them, performance goals, and the importance of those goals. When *management* defines those four things, individuals develop external commitment to the organization and to the work. If Argyris is right—and we tend to think that he is—it does not take a rocket scientist to understand that the fundamental reason why participatory models fail is because individuals in many organizations are not truly empowered to participate in the meaningful ways required. Given that, the bigger and more fundamental question becomes, "Why do organizations find it so difficult for employees to develop internal commitment to the organization? Why is it so hard to truly empower the employee?"

The Argyris analysis finds fault on both sides of the table. He believes that many executives—consciously or unconsciously—undermine empowerment, perhaps because they are unsure that they truly want empowerment. Instead, executives seem to prefer to "anoint champions" who will pursue objectives within carefully controlled change programs. When the rank and file is not truly free to create the tasks, goals, and behaviors, it is not empowered—and internal commitment does not emerge.

On the other hand, Argyris points out that employees also have their doubts, because it can be threatening and bewildering for individuals to buy into the new programs. Workers often use external commitment as a survival tactic that permits individuals to negotiate what they experience as a hostile and uncaring environment. Argyris says that offering employees rewards tends to make them dependent. An offer of genuine empowerment can seem to thwart the acquisition of the desired rewards.

As Argyris puzzles over the solution to this situation, he arrives at a critique of the efficacy of empowerment itself. This much-needed analysis of the ultimate viability of empowerment models tends in our view, however, to fall short in its final thrust. After suggesting such solutions as the organization establishing working conditions that genuinely encourage internal commitment and that all companies need mechanisms for top-down control as well as bottom-up participation, he admonishes us to do the following:

> Finally, remember that empowerment can run contrary to human nature, and be realistic about how to achieve it. To paraphrase Abraham Lincoln: You can empower all of the people some of the time and some of the people all of the time, but you can't empower all of the people all of the time. (p. 105)

While (along with Argyris and others) we appreciate the disappointments experienced as a result of the numerous failures around the country of participatory-empowerment strategies, we cannot share the conclusion that empowerment might be contrary to human nature. Rather, as we have attempted to demonstrate here, we think many of the failures have resulted because the implementation strategies ran counter not to human nature, but to American culture and the primacy of the individual within the culture.

PERSON-CENTERED POSSIBILITIES

A person-centered approach is different from other sorts of participatory and empowerment approaches. Yes, employees participate, and yes, they are empowered. But in addition, employees receive the message that their personal and professional development is just as important as the organization's mission. In fact, the organization is construed to have a dual mission: the development of the individual employee and the stated product or service goal.

A Fundamental Difference

Within typical empowerment models that are not person centered, employees are enabled to make key decisions about the goals, processes, and commitments of the organization. Employees become the experts, and their opinions carry weight. In person-centered empowerment settings, however, there is as much emphasis on individual growth agendas as there is on the organization's goals. People make decisions about what is good for them as well as what is good for the company. As one corporate leader pointed out, associates within this model come to merge their own goals with that of the company, because personal growth and company growth are not at odds. In fact, they have merged (Arnold & Plas, 1993). In an individualist society, this sort of model fits well. The individual expects responsibilities and opportunities.

NONPROFIT ORGANIZATIONS AND PERSON-CENTERED POSSIBLITIES

Burnout has been considered one of the leading inhibitors of quality performance within organizations (Barrett, Riggar, Flowers, Crimando, & Bailey, 1997; Cherniss, 1995; & Maslach, 1997). The history of nonprofit management that we reviewed in Chapter 1, "Common Ground," leads to the conclusion that a remarkably new approach to nonprofit management might be needed. When the challenges are as great as they are within most social-service organizations, only an outstanding management model can provide the opportunity for quality service. Trying to effectively cope with poverty, disease, crime, and alienation is one of the most difficult jobs anywhere in organizational America. People who labor in these jobs need the best leadership and management support that is available today.

Person-Centered Nonprofit Leadership

Person-centered leadership seems uniquely suited to nonprofit organizations. When focus, energy, and resources are channeled toward the individual associate, that employee is much better equipped to bring the community's resources to bear on the human problems that demand solutions. Oasis Center, the case study we presented here, has demonstrated for a number of years what the payoffs can be when a person-centered leadership approach develops within a social-service agency.

The Oasis Center's Unique Person-Centered Model

We pointed out throughout this book that Oasis Center is by no means a faultless organization. Oasis has strengths and weaknesses, just like all other organizations. The associates at this agency make mistakes. Some days bring out the worst in them. Some situations overwhelm them and tax them to their limits. They do not claim perfection for themselves. Our study did not reveal them to be a perfect organization.

What can be said about Oasis is that it has developed—and now maintains—a leadership and management model that results in high-quality service, a proliferation of creative and effective programs, community, regional, and national recognition and support, and most importantly, reduced levels of burnout and significant client change. The conclusion is warranted that Oasis achieves these successes because it invests significantly in the individual employee.

The Oasis Future

Clearly, this organization is not the same one that we studied in the mid-1990s. The differences are quite apparent. There have been changes in board relationships, organizational culture, team relations, and staff composition. But fundamentally (and most obvious) is that the programmatic focus of the center has broadened. While throughout the previous decades the center had been committed to assisting the development of troubled teens, that is no longer what this agency is all about exclusively. Now, a youth-leadership agenda also exists.

Community Development

Programs have grown, and the staff has grown in skills as well as in size. Increased growth is not the biggest story, however. The mission of the organization has changed to a much more public mission. Oasis is now heavily committed to community development on behalf of the community's teen population. In fact, this focus is now primary in the center. So, a substantial portion of the organization's efforts are driven by prevention issues, rather than issues of developmental delay or dysfunction.

An example of the new directions is that Oasis has been instrumental in helping to establish a youth advisory council to the mayor. A popular and successful community event each summer on Thursday evenings called Dancin' in the District attracted thousands of Nashville's teens to the downtown area, where they mingle with 20- and 30-something singles in an alcohol and music venue. Teen alcohol abuse became a problem. Many in the community were outraged. The situation threatened to develop into an atmosphere of hostility toward youth. Oasis staffers worked with others around town to take advantage of this situation to create a voice for teens in their own community. Problems were resolved. More importantly, however, teens gained the mayor's ear and the attention of the community as a responsible constituency worth recognizing.

At the time of this writing, many staffers at Oasis consider the youth-development agenda to be the biggest part of their daily work. A sizable percentage of the associates work within programs that have a substantial prevention and development component. People now keep a tight focus on the possibility that the community can change certain key factors that are capable of controlling the growth of teen violence, gangs, and the individual dysfunction that tends to result when families do not have the emotional resources necessary to help their teens gain a strong sense of self and self-respect.

Progress in Development of the Leadership Model

This organization has developed person-centered empowerment, where individuals are encouraged to set goals for themselves as well as for the organization. They make decisions about what is best for them as well as what is best for the organization and its clients. Their model frees them to participate fully. The model makes it possible for them to dream—not only about the futures of their clients, but also about the possibilities for the development of humankind. Yes, while we have heretofore been somewhat reluctant to mention it, the reality is that Oasis associates commonly tend to take their place in society rather seriously. They speculate about developments in social evolution. They think out loud about the roles that they and their organization can possibly play in shaping the future of the Nashville community, the state, and the steady, positive progress of people in general. We have not mentioned this phenomenon prior to this concluding moment, because being the sort of objective researchers that we have been trained to be, we did not want to paint a picture that might suggest that this agency is not for real. We worried that you might think these people to be a little too good to be true.

Yet, our honest impression has been that these individuals are not a great deal different than others we have known within the nonprofit field. Each has arrived at Oasis as a fairly typical, well-trained sort of social-service worker. In contrast to workers in other social-service agencies (Geurts, Schaufeli, & DeJonge, 1998; & Krakinowski, 1992), however, these associates do not slide the slippery slope toward burnout; rather, they turn the other way. After some time, they have tended to change in the directions we have described throughout this book. As the organization grew, so did the individual. Associates claim that the management system enables them to bring forth the best from themselves, including a heightened sense of their responsibilities to their country and even to humanity in general.

Results of our five year study have supported the conclusions that individual associates have reached: that the Oasis management model frees people to do better and more creative work and to suffer fewer negative personal consequences that are often associated with labor in this field.

IN CONCLUSION

The possibilities for effective, person-centered nonprofit management might be limited only by the number of agencies that choose to develop such a participatory model. That is to say, each nonprofit, person-centered leadership story will be a unique story. No two interpretations of the model can—nor should be expected to—be alike. The nature of the philosophy and strategies ensures that each successful version of the model will be a reflection of the specific people who compose that organization.

While the Oasis model is but one approach to person-centered empowerment, theirs has been, for us, a particularly interesting organization to study and a particularly rewarding story to tell. In fact, we will watch the Oasis future with great interest and great admiration. What started as an investigation of the possibilities of person-centered, nonprofit leadership somewhere along the line became for us, in addition, a grateful acknowledgement of the privilege it has been to study this sort of outstanding organization. Oasis makes a difference and changes lives. Along with thousands of happier kids and their families, we salute these remarkable people who day after day do what they set out to do what this community wants them to do: the improbable and the impossible.

REFERENCES

Argyris, C. (1998). Empowerment: The emperor's new clothes. *Harvard Business Review*, Volume 76, pp. 98–105.

Arnold, W. W. and Plas, J. M. (1993). *The human touch: Today's most unusual program for productivity and profit*. New York: John Wiley & Sons, Inc.

Barrett, K., Riggar, T. F., Flowers, C. R., Crimando, W., and Bailey, T. (1997). The turnover dilemma: A disease with solutions. *Journal of Rehabilitation*, Volume 63, pp. 36–44.

Blanchard, K. H., Carlos, J. P., and Randolph, A. (1999). *The three keys to empowerment: Release the power within people for astonishing results*. San Francisco: Berrett-Kohler.

Block. P. (1987). *The empowered manager*. San Francisco: Jossey-Bass.

Bracey, H., Rosenblum, J., Sanford, A., and Trueblood, R. (1990). *Managing from the heart*.

Cherniss, C. (1995). *Beyond burnout: Helping teachers, nurses, therapists, and lawyers recover from stress and disillusionment*. New York: Routledge.

Deal, T. and Kennedy, A. (1999). *The new corporate cultures*. Reading, MA: Perseus Press.

Geurts, S., Schaufeli, W., and DeJonge, J. (1998). Burnout and intention to leave among mental health-care professionals: A social psychological approach. *Journal of Social and Clinical Psychology*, Volume 17, pp. 341–362.

Krakinowski, L. (1992). Preventing burnout. *Rehabilitation Today*, Volume 2, pp. 18–23.

Mann, N. R. (1989). *The keys to excellence* (3rd ed.). Los Angeles: Prestwick.

Maslach, C. and Leiter, M. P. (1997). *The truth about burnout: How organizations cause personal stress and what to do about it*. San Francisco: Jossey-Bass.

Pitt, H. (1994). *SPC for the rest of us*. Reading, MA: Addison-Wesley.

Reina, D. S. and Reina, M. L. (1999). *Trust and betrayal in the workplace*. San Francisco: Berrett-Kohler.

Schrage, M. (1995). The rules of collaboration. *Forbes ASAP*, Volume 155, pp. 88–89.

Whitney, J. (1994). *The trust factor: Liberating profits and restoring corporate vitality*. New York: McGraw-Hill.

Appendix
Methods

The research project that formed the basis of this book developed from the combined interests and expertise of the authors. Jeanne Plas has studied and written extensively about person-centered management in the for-profit sector of corporate America. Susan Lewis's background is in non-profit management, and she serves as a consultant to a number of nonprofit boards. The authors had collaborated on a methodologically similar project, studying sense of community in a planned town. The outstanding reputation of Oasis Center was well known to both investigators, and they determined to apply systematic, qualitative research to discover the reasons behind Oasis's success.

The qualitative approach used was based on the methodological thinking of Lincoln and Guba (1985). Within this research model, inquiry cycles and recycles through four methodological stages that involve sampling, inductive analysis, theory development, and development of next steps based on what has been discovered to that point. The longitudinal project reported here had three distinct phases. The first and foundational phase spanned an 18- to 24-month period. During that time, the four methodological stages mentioned previously were employed, then repeated. The organization was investigated again after a period of about 18 months. We undertook a third investigational phase one year after that.

Primary data collection was completed in 1994 and 1995 and came from two sources:

1. In-depth interviews of staff members representing all agency teams, board members, other community agencies interfacing with Oasis (such as Juvenile Justice), and clients and their families.

2. Participant observer field notes from Lewis, who served as an intern in the shelter during the study. One-third of the interviews were conducted with both investigators present in order to ensure reliability in administering the qualitative protocol. One or the other of the researchers conducted the remaining interviews. The interview was a semi-structured protocol that began with open-ended questions regarding the strengths and weaknesses of the agency. The questions were designed to cover a number of specific probes regarding the agency and its functioning but enabled the interview to proceed largely in response to informant comments.

Additionally, Lewis served as an intern at Oasis during part of the investigative period. Her dual roles were clear to staff members, and the function that she was serving was understood each time she was in the agency. The internship enabled her to undertake the research function of participant observer, interacting with the ongoing activities of the Shelter Program, attending staff meetings of both the Shelter Team and the agency at large, and participating in agency fundraising activities, staff retreats, and special events.

The second phase of data collection occurred across a six-month period in 1997 and 1998. As was the case in the first phase, primary data-collection methods involved qualitative interviews involving individual and group sessions with staff and board members. The final stage of data collection, conducted during the summer of 1999, also relied on individual and group interviews.

Through the auspices of The Oasis Center, all research participants who are quoted in this book agreed that their names and comments could be used. None of the quotes are from informal conversations with Lewis as an intern, although that perspective has provided general confirmatory data to the information from the formal interviews.

REFERENCE

Lincoln, Y. S., & Guba, E. (1985) *Naturalistic inquiry*. Beverly Hills, CA; Sage.

Index

acceptance (Oasis Center model), 77
Alternative Spring Break program
    (Oasis Center), 60
attitudes (Oasis Center staff), 123-125

Board of Directors
    Oasis Center meeting, 123, 125-126
        communication patters, 128-130
        follow-up with staff, 127-128
        problem resolutions, 131-132
        staff point of view, 123-125
Board Team
    Oasis Center structure, 56
burnout
    communication needs, 20
    history of, 7-8
    low levels of (Oasis Center
        strengths), 119
    low salaries, 102-103
    Oasis Center model and
        empowerment, 84-85
    organizational change effects, 12
    participatory management
        benefits, 13
    prevention strategies, 11
    research findings, 9-10

collegiality (Oasis Center shelter
    program), 138
communication
    cultural traps, 100-102
    dealing with problems, 108-109
    patterns (Oasis Center board
        meeting), 128-132
    traditional management, 19-20
        nonprofit implications, 20
community (Oasis Center teams),
    155-156
confrontation, productive (Oasis
    Center model), 78-81
counseling, outpatient (Oasis
    Center), 59
Counseling Team (Oasis Center
    structure), 56
creativity
    Oasis Center program
        strengths, 116
    Oasis Center shelter program,
        140-141
crisis call lines (Oasis Center), 58
culture (Oasis Center), 55
    leadership philosophy, 66
    model framework, 65
    weaknesses, 100-102

decision-making (Oasis Center
    weaknesses), 98
Educational Services Team (Oasis
    Center structure), 57
ELECT program (Oasis Center), 60
employees
    empowering, 27
        psychological contexts, 28-29
        worker participation, history of,
            29-30
    Oasis Center growth philosophy, 74
    pressure upon, 5-7
        burnout, 7-11
        organizational change effects, 12
        participatory management
            benefits, 13
employment, youth (Oasis Center), 60
empowerment
    employee, 27
        psychological contexts, 28-29
        worker participation, history of,
            29-30
    Oasis Center model, 81
        and burnout, 84-85
        personal, 83-84
        professional, 82
        youth, 85
executive directors (communication
    roles), 129

Family Retreat Team (Oasis Center
    structure), 57
family retreat weekends (Oasis
    Center), 60
family support (Oasis Center), 75-77
Family Weekend Retreat (Oasis Center
    model), 70-73
flexibility (Oasis Center)
    shelter program, 140-141
    teams, 152
for-profit organizations (traditional
    management models), 64
funding, 61
    dealing with problems, 107-108

inexperience in, 105-107
low salaries, 102-103
scarcity models, 104-105

goals, clarifying (teamwork), 151
groups
    making decisions (Oasis Center
        weaknesses), 98
    vs. teams (Oasis Center), 149-150
growth (Oasis Center teams), 151
history (Oasis Center), 61
improvement (Oasis Center shelter
    program), 142-144
improving quality, 25-26
individuals (Oasis Center model)
    acceptance, 77
    commitment to development, 67-70
    cultural roles, 37-38
    employee growth philosophy, 74
    empowerment, 81-85
    family support, 75-77
    productive confrontation, 78-81
    team-building, 86-87
inexperience with funding issues,
    105-107

leaders, team (Oasis Center), 148-149
leadership, 23
    management comparisons, 23
        participatory management, 24
    Oasis Center (culture as
        philosophy), 66
    Oasis Center shelter program, 137
    person-centered, 35
        future of, 159-165
        individuals, roles of, 37-38
        models, how they work, 40-42
        person-centered management, 44
        servant leadership comparisons,
            43-44
        teamwork, 36-37, 39
locations (Oasis Center), 52-53

management, 21-22
  leadership comparisons, 23
    participatory management, 24
  participatory, 24
    employees, empowering, 27-30
    hiring a learning workforce, 27
    history of, 25-26
    Japanese perspectives, 26
    Oasis Center shelter program,
      139-142
    person-centered leadership, 35-44
    quality improvement goals, 26
  person-centered
    future of, 159-165
    person-centered leadership
      comparisons, 44
  traditional models, 19, 64
  communication problems, 19-20
Management Team (Oasis Center
  structure), 57
mistakes, handling (Oasis Center
  teams), 152
models (Oasis person-centered model),
  40-42, 63
    acceptance, 77
    commitment to individual
      development, 67-70
    culture as leadership
      philosophy, 66
    culture as model framework, 65
    employee growth philosophy, 74
    empowerment, 81-85
    family support, 75-77
    Family Weekend Retreat, 70-73
    meeting staff needs, 64
    productive confrontation, 78-81
    starting the process, 88
    team-building, 86-87
morale
  low salaries, 102-103
  Oasis Center shelter program,
    133-135
    collegiality, 138
    continuing improvement, 142-144
    creativity, 140-141

    daily challenges, 135-136
    downsides to participatory
      management, 139-140
    leadership that listens, 137
    respect and caring, 142

nonprofit organizations
  communication needs, 20
  future of, 159-165
  history of, 14-15
  Oasis Center, 51-52
    Board Team, 56
    Counseling Team, 56
    culture, 55
    Educational Services Team, 57
    Family Retreat Team, 57
    funding, 61
    history of, 61
    location, 52-53
    Management Team, 57
    philosophy, 55
    programs, 58-60
    Shelter Team, 58
    Support Team, 58
    Transitional Living Team, 57
    work and benefit examples, 53-55
  participatory management, moving
    to, 64

Oasis Center, 51-52
  Board of Directors meeting, 123,
    125-126
    communication patterns, 128-130
    follow-up with staff, 127-128
    problem resolutions, 131-132
    staff point of view, 123-125
  culture, 55
  funding, 61
  future of, 159-165
  history of, 61
  infrastructure
    Board Team, 56
    Counseling Team, 56

Educational Services Team, 57
Family Retreat Team, 57
Management Team, 57
Shelter Team, 58
Support Team, 58
Transitional Living Team, 57
location, 52-53
longitudinal methodology, 95-97
person-centered model, 63
  acceptance, 77
  commitment to individual
    development, 67-70
  culture as leadership
    philosophy, 66
  culture as model framework, 65
  employee growth philosophy, 74
  empowerment, 81-85
  family support, 75-77
  Family Weekend Retreat, 70-73
  meeting staff needs, 64
  productive confrontation, 78-81
  starting the process, 88
  team-building, 86-87
philosophy, 55
programs, 58-60
shelter program
  collegiality, 138
  continuing improvement, 142-144
  creativity, 140-141
  daily challenges, 135-136
  downside to participatory
    management, 139-140
  leadership that listens, 137
  negative circumstances, 133-135
  respect and caring, 142
strengths, 113
  burnout-free environment, 119
  clients get better, 113-116
  commitment to staff
    development, 117-119
  creative response to community
    need, 116
  local and national reputation, 116
teamwork, 147-148
  community, sense of, 155-156
  flexibility, 152

goal clarity, 151
groups vs. teams, 149-150
individual and collective
    growth, 151
mistakes, handling, 152
strengths within vs. between
    teams, 153-154
team leaders, 148-149
trusting relationships, 152
weaknesses, organizational,
    154-155
weaknesses, 99
  communication problems,
    108-109
  cultural traps, 100-102
  funding issues, 107-108
  inexperience with funding
    issues, 105-107
  low salaries, 102-103
  making group decisions, 98
  over-emphasis on, 110-112
  scarcity models, 104-105
  work and benefit examples, 53-55
organization
  cultural traps, 100-102
  Oasis Center
    Board Team, 56
    Counseling Team, 56
    Educational Services Team, 57
    Family Retreat Team, 57
    longitudinal methodology, 95-97
    Management Team, 57
    Shelter Team, 58
    Support Team, 58
    Transitional Living Team, 57
outcomes, Oasis Center (clients get
    better), 113-116
outpatient counseling (Oasis Center), 59

participatory boards, 131-132
participatory management, 24
  employees, empowering, 27-29
    worker participation, history of,
      29-30

hiring a learning workforce, 27
history of, 25-26
  Japanese perspectives, 26
moving to, 64
Oasis Center shelter program
  continuing improvement, 142-144
  creativity, 140-141
  downsides, 139-140
  respect and caring, 142
Oasis person-centered model, 63
  acceptance, 77
  commitment to individual
    development, 67-70
  culture as leadership
    philosophy, 66
  culture as model framework, 65
  employee growth philosophy, 74
  empowerment, 81-85
  family support, 75-77
  Family Weekend Retreat, 70-73
  meeting staff needs, 64
  productive confrontation, 78-81
  starting the process, 88
  team-building, 86-87
person-centered leadership, 35
  individuals, roles of, 37-38
  models, how they work, 40-42
  person-centered management
    comparisons, 44
  servant leadership comparisons,
    43-44
  teamwork, 36-37, 39
quality improvement goals, 26
patterns, communication (Oasis Center
  board meeting), 128-132
person-centered leadership, 35
  future of, 159-165
  individuals, roles of, 37-38
  models, how they work, 40-42
  person-centered management
    comparisons, 44
  servant leadership comparisons,
    43-44
  teamwork, 36-37, 39
    sports teams, 39
    work teams, 39

personal empowerment (Oasis Center
  model), 83-84
philosophies (Oasis Center), 55
pressure, 5-7
  burnout
    communication needs, 20
    history of, 7-8
    prevention strategies, 11
    research findings, 9-10
  organizational change effects, 12
  participatory management
    benefits, 13
preventing burnout, 11
  participatory management
    benefits, 13
problems, resolving (participatory
  boards), 131-132
productive confrontation (Oasis Center
  model), 78-81
products, quality, improving, 25-26
professional empowerment (Oasis
  Center model), 82
programs (Oasis Center), 58-60
  strengths, 116
PULSE community volunteer
  programs (Oasis Center), 60

quality
  improvement vs. assurance, 25
  improving, 26
reputations (Oasis Center), 116
research (studying burnout), 9-10
respect (Oasis Center shelter
  program), 142
salaries, low levels of (Oasis Center
  weaknesses), 102-103
scarcity models, funding problems,
  104-105
  inexperience, 105-107
servant leadership comparisons, 43-44
service providers (pressures), 5-7
  burnout, 7-11
  organizational change effects, 12
  participatory management
    benefits, 13

shelter program (Oasis Center), 59
  collegiality, 138
  continuing improvement, 142-144
  creativity, 140-141
  daily challenges, 135-136
  downsides to participatory
    management, 139-140
  leadership that listens, 137
  negative circumstances, 133-135
  respect and caring, 142
Shelter Team (Oasis Center
  structure), 58
social-service management, history of,
  14-15
sports teams (teamwork examples), 39
staff (Oasis Center), meeting their
  needs, 64
  commitment to development,
    117-119
street outreach programs (Oasis
  Center), 58
strengths
  Oasis Center, 113
    burnout-free environment, 119
    clients get better, 113-116
    commitment to staff
      development, 117-119
    creative response to community
      need, 116
    local and national reputation, 116
  within vs. between Oasis teams,
    153-154
suggestion boxes, 19
Support Team (Oasis Center
  structure), 58

teamwork, 36-39
  inter-team communication
    problems, 108-109
  Oasis Center model (team-building),
    86-87

Oasis Center teams, 147-148
  community, sense of, 155-156
  flexibility, 152
  goal clarity, 151
  groups vs. teams, 149-150
  individual and collective
    growth, 151
  mistakes, handling, 152
  strengths within vs. between
    teams, 153-154
  team leaders, 148-149
  trusting relationships, 152
  weaknesses, organizational,
    154-155
sports teams, 39
work teams, 39
Teen Outreach Program (Oasis
  Center), 60
traditional management, 19
  communication problems, 19-20
  nonprofit implications, 20
Transitional Living Team, 59
  Oasis Center structure, 57
trust (Oasis Center teams), 152

weaknesses (Oasis Center), 99
  communication problems, 108-109
  cultural traps, 100-102
  funding issues, 107-108
  inexperience with funding issues,
    105-107
  low salaries, 102-103
  making group decisions, 98
  over-emphasis on, 110-112
  scarcity models, 104-105
  teams (organizational), 154-155
youth employment (Oasis Center), 60
youth empowerment (Oasis Center
  model), 85

About the Authors

Jeanne M. Plas, PhD, is a member of the Psychology and Human Development faculty at Vanderbilt University, where she has been associated with clinical, school, and community psychology training programs for 25 years. Her research and theoretical writings on leadership and emotions in the workplace have received national and international recognition and praise. Two of her best-selling leadership and management books, *Working Up a Storm: Anger, Anxiety, Joy, and Tears on the Job* (1989) and *The Human Touch* (1993) have been translated into Portuguese and Chinese, while English editions of her work have been distributed in more than 12 countries. Dr. Plas has been a consultant to such U.S. organizations as General Motors (GM), the California Financial and Banking Network, Dow Jones & Co., and the United States Army. Internationally, she has been a consultant to diverse groups such as Newfoundland Light and Power and the Brothers of Charity in Ireland. She has studied numerous person-centered organizations with widely dissimilar interests, such as advertising, urban planning, social services, public utilities, manufacturing, industrial support, and government. A recent book, *Person-Centered Leadership* (1996), has been used as a participatory-management textbook in a variety of learning-organization settings as well as in business and industrial psychology programs. She has discussed her work in many major U.S. business magazines and newspapers, such as *The Wall Street Journal* and *Business Week*, as well as in major newspapers throughout the world.

At Vanderbilt, Dr. Plas currently teaches advanced seminars in organizational leadership and courses in sports leadership, research methods and adult development. In Ohio, Dr. Plas can be reached at (440) 458-8361 (1852 Grafton Rd., Elyria, OH 44035). In Tennessee she can be reached at (615) 322-8147 (Box 512, GPC Station, Vanderbilt University, Nashville, TN 37203) or through e-mail at jeanne.plas@vanderbilt.edu.

Susan E. Lewis, MS, is completing her dissertation within the Community Psychology program at Vanderbilt University. Her research and writing efforts have been directed toward nonprofit management as well as issues related to sense of community and family studies. Lewis gained 13 years of hands-on experience as chief executive officer of an international women's nonprofit organization and subsequently conducted numerous training programs in leadership development and strategic planning for nonprofit organizations. She was named a fellow by the American Society of Association Executives in 1987 as one of 11 top association executives in the country. Lewis is also a practicing marriage and family therapist and has served as dean of students at Huntingdon College in Montgomery, Alabama. She lives in Franklin, Tennessee with her husband and has two grown children, each of whom are pursuing their respective dreams. Ms. Lewis can be reached at 615-591-7420 (401 Chamberlain Park Lane, Franklin, TN 37069) or through e-mail at susan.k.lewis@vanderbilt.edu.